SCOTTISH TRADES ᴜ.ᴜɴᴜ

A Selected Bibliography

[Including a summary of Scottish Directories]

by

D. Richard Torrance

for

The Scottish Association of Family History
Societies

1991

CONTENTS

****

ADDRESSES OF THE PRINCIPAL SCOTTISH LIBRARIES

Aberdeenshire

Aberdeen Central Library
Rosemount Viaduct
Aberdeen
AB9 1GU

Argyll & Bute

District Library H Q
Hunter Street
Kirn
Dunoon
Argyll
PA23 8JR

Ayrshire

Carnegie Library Ayr
12 Main Street
Ayr
KA8 8ED

Cunninghame District Library
39-41 Princes Street
Ardrossan
Ayrshire
KA22 8BT

Cumnock & Doon Valley
District Library
Bank Glen
Cumnock
KA18 1PH

Kilmarnock & Loudon
District Libraries
Dick Institute
14 Elmbank Avenue
Kilmarnock
KA1 3BL

Banffshire

Peterhead Public Library
apply to:
N.E. Scotland Library Service
14 Crown Terrace
Aberdeen
AB9 2BH

Berwickshire

Duns Area Library apply to:
Borders District Library
St Mary's Mill
Selkirk
TD7 3EU

Dumbartonshire

Dumbarton Branch Library
Levenford House
Strathleven Place
Dumbarton
G82 1BD

Strathkelvin District Libraries
Reference Department
William Patrick
Memorial Library
Camphill Avenue
Kirkintilloch
G66 1DW

Dumfriesshire

Ewart Library
Catherine Street
Dumfries
DG1 1JB

Fife

Dunfermline District Libraries
1 Abbot Street
Dunfermline
KY12 7NL

Kirkcaldy Central Library
War Memorial Grounds
Kirkcaldy
KY1 1YG

Methil Public Library
Wellesley Road
Methil
KY8 3PA

North East Fife
District Library
County Buildings
St Catherine's Street
Cupar
KY15 4TM

Forfarshire

Angus Libraries & Museums
County Buildings
Forfar
DD8 3LG

Arbroath Library
Hill Terrace
Arbroath
DD11 1AJ

Brechin Public Library
St Ninian's Square
Brechin
Angus
DD9 7AA

William Coull Anderson
Library of Geneaolgy
Dewar House
Hill Terrace
Arbroath
DD11 1DB

Dundee Central Library
The Wellgate
Dundee
DD1 1BB

Forfar Public Library
West High Street
Forfar
Angus
DD8 1BB

Inverness-shire

The Library
Farraline Park
Inverness
IV1 1LS

Lanarkshire

Lanark Library
Lindsay Institute
Hope Street
Lanark
ML11 7LZ

Bearsden & Milngavie
District Libraries
Brockwood
166 Drymen Road
Bearsden
Glasgow
G61 3RJ

Coatbridge Library
Academy Street
Coatbridge
ML5 3AT

Hamilton Library
98 Cadzow Street
Hamilton
ML3 6HQ

Mitchell Library
North Street
Glasgow
G3 7DN

Motherwell Library
Hamilton Road
Motherwell
ML1 3BZ

Lothians

National Library of Scotland
George IV Bridge
Edinburgh
EH1 1EW

Edinburgh Central Library
George IV Bridge
Edinburgh
EH1

Scottish Record Office
Princes Street
Edinburgh
EH1   3YJ

The Court of the Lord Lyon
General Register House
Princes Street
Edinburgh
EH1 3YT

National Library of Scotland
Map Room
33 Salisbury Place
Edinburgh
EH9 1SL

The Scottish Genealogy Society
Library & Family History Centre
15 Victoria Terrace
Edinburgh
EH1 2JL

The Scottish United Services
Museum Library.
Museum Square
The Castle
Edinburgh
EH1   2NG

Midlothian District Library
7 Station Road
Roslin
Midlothian
EH25 9PF

East Lothian District Library
Library Headquarters
Lodge Street
Haddington
EH41 3DX

West Lothian District Libraries
Wellpark
66 Marjoriebanks Street
Bathgate
EH48 1AN

Morayshire

Moray District Council
Department of Libraries
Elgin Library
Grant Lodge
Cooper Park
Elgin
IV30 1HS

Orkney

The Orkney Library
Laing Street
Kirkwall
Orkney
KW15 1NW

Peeblesshire

Peebles Area Library
apply to:-
Borders Regional Library
St Mary's Mill
Selkirk
TD7 3EV

Perthshire

Sandeman Library
Kinnoull Street
Perth
PH1 5ET

Renfrewshire

Paisley Central Library
High Street
Paisley
PA1 2BB

Eastwood District Libraries
Council Offices
Eastwood Park
Rouken Glen Road
Giffnock
Glasgow
G46 6UG

Inverclyde District Libraries
Watt Library
9 Union Street
Greenock
PA16 8JH

Ross & Cromarty

Western Isles Library
2 Keith Street
Stornoway
Isle of Lewis
PA87 2QG

Roxburghshire

Hawick Library &
Kelso Branch Library
apply to:-
Borders Regional Library
St Mary's Mill
Selkirk
TD7 3EV

Selkirkshire

Galashiels Area Library
apply to:-
Borders Regional Library
St Mary's Mill
Selkirk
TD7 3EV

Shetland

Shetland Library
Lower Hillhead
Lerwick
Shetland
ZE1 0EL

Stirlingshire

Falkirk Library
Hope Street
Falkirk
FK1 5AU

Stirling Central Library
Corn Exchange Road
Stirling
FK8 2HX

Stirling District Library HQ
Borrowmead Road
Springkerse Industrial Estate
Stirling
FK7 7TN

Western Isles

Western Isles Library H Q
Keith Street
Stornoway
Isle of Lewis
PA87 2QG

Wigtown

Stranraer Branch Library
London Road
Stranraer
DG9 8ES

REST OF BRITAIN

British Library
Dept. of Printed Books
Great Russell Street
London
WC1B 3DG

The British Library
Oriental & India Office
Collections
197 Blackfriars Road
London
SE1 8NG

Bodleian Library
Unviersity of Oxford
Broad Street
Oxford
OX1 3BG

Guildhall Library
Aldermanbury
London
EC2P 2EJ

National Library of Wales
Aberystwyth
Dyfed
SY23 3BU

University Library Cambridge
West Road
Cambridge
CB3 9DR

INDEX

of

DIRECTORIES, TRADES AND PROFESSIONS

SCOTTISH TRADES & PROFESSIONS

A Bibliography

Introduction

As interest in genealogy and family history grows researchers are increasingly trying to find more background information to their ancestors' lives.

Although many people worked on the land very little has been published about them. There are various general descriptions of agriculture and more is to be found in the three statistical accounts.

As one starts to search for material connected with trade in the Scottish burghs the volume of references works increases substantially, although the amount of published work varies from burgh to burgh and in some cases seems to have been dependant on one or two enthusiasts transcribing records and getting them published.

As far as possible works have been quoted which contain lists of individuals. In many cases the works list only office bearers, but they do give useful background detail on the trade or profession.

By their nature, many of the volumes mentioned are quite scarce and it will be necessary to consult the library of the burgh or region about which the book deals. However, it is possible to find some of these volumes in second hand book dealers reasonably priced.

DIRECTORIES

Below is a summary of most of the Scottish Directories available to the researcher. The first section deals with works which relate to the whole of Scotland or large areas of Scotland. The second, larger section, covers Scotland county by county.

The title and years covered by the series are given. Some, like the Post Office Directories, are fairly readily available, but others are quite scarce. With the scarcer volumes the area to which they refer is the best area to seek them out. A list of addresses of the main Scottish libraries is to be found at the front of this volume.

General

A Directory of Landownership in Scotland, c. 1770. Ed. L.R. Timperley, 1976, for the Scottish Record Society.

Bailey's Northern Directory, or Merchants' and Tradesmen's Useful Companion for 1781. [covers Edinburgh, Leith, Glasgow, Paisley, Greenock & Port Glasgow].

British National Directory, 1781 - 1819: an index to places in the British Isles including a trades directory with general provincial coverage. Ian Maxted, Exeter, 1989.

Merchants Directory or Lex Mercateria. Thomas Mortimer. 1783. [A complete guide to all men in business with an account of our Mercantile Companies, colonies, factories abroad, Commercial Treaties with foreign powers, the duty of Consuls and of the law concerning aliens, naturalisation and denization].

Travellers' Directory through Scotland. [1792, reprinted 1798].

The British Almanack & Glasgow Register. [1806].

The General Almanack of Scotland & British Regions. [1809 - 1814].

The Commercial Directory of Ireland, Scotland and the four northern most counties of England for 1820, 1821 & 1822. [1820]

Pigot & Co's National Commercial Directory of the whole of Scotland and the Isle of Man. [1821, 1825, 1837].

The Circulation of the Edinburgh, Leith, Glasgow & North British Commercial Advertiser. [1827].

The Angus & Mearns Commercial & Agricultural Rememberancer. [1829 - 1851; 9 vols.]

The Angus & Mearns County Rememberancer. [1836].

Directory to Noblemen and Gentlemens' Seats, Villages in Scotland. [1843, 1852, 1857].

The Angus & Mearns Directory. [1845, 1847].

2

Slater's Royal National Commercial Directory and Topography of Scotland. [1843 - 1915;].

Valuation Rolls. These are available for the whole of Scotland from 1855. They give information about ownership, tenancy, values and rents of land and houses. The Scottish Record Office holds these, but they will need to be consulted personally. It would be worth checking local libraries and record offices to see what they hold.

Morton's New Farmers' Almanac. [1860]. Then:- Morton's Almanac for farmers & landowners. [1873 - 1887]. Then:- Vinter's Agricultural annual. [1907 - 1924].

The County Directory of Scotland. [1862 - 1912; 10 vols.].

The Southern Counties Register and Directory for Roxburgh, Berwick and Selkirk. [1866; facsimile reprint 1990].

The Commercial Directory of Glasgow and the West of Scotland. [1870, 1872, 1874].

Glasgow, Greenock, Edinburgh & Leith Commercial List. [1873 - 1874]. continued as: The Scotch Commercial List. [1876 - 1900].

The Poor Law Directory for Scotland. [1874].

Owners of Lands & Heritages 1872 - 1873 (Scotland). Accounts & Papers, 43 vols. (38 pt III), Session 5.3.1874 - 7.8.1874.

The Border Almanac. [1875 - 1917].

The Pocket Commercial Gazetteer of Scotland. [1877].

Worrall's Directory of the North Eastern Counties of Scotland comprising - Forfar, Fife, Kinross, Aberdeen, Banff and Kincardine. [1877].

Macdonald's Scottish Directory and Gazetteer. [1884 - 1973].

Clark's Trades & Professions Directory for the counties of Forfar, Perth & Fife. [1885].

The West Coast Almanack and Business Directory. [1883 - 1886].

The West Coast Illustrated Commercial Almanac, Calendar, Diary & Business Directory. [1883 - 1885].

Parochial Directory of Scotland. [1877 - 1897].

Ayrshire, Dumfriesshire, Wigtownshire and Kirkcudbrightshire Business Directory. [1893].

Fifeshire, Clackmannanshire and Kinross-shire Business Directory. [1893].

Roxburghshire, Selkirkshire, Peebleshire and Berwickshire Business Directory. [1893].

Stirlingshire, Dunbartonshire and Linlithgowshire Business Directory. [1893].

Sells Directory of Telegraphic Addresses. [1895 - 1967].

The Local Government Directory of Scotland. [1895 - 1933].

Clarke's Business Directory of Scotland. [1895 & 1898].

The Border Counties - Business Directory. [1897, 3rd ed.].

Collin's Business Directory of Scotland. [1899].

Edinburgh and South of Scotland Trades Directory. [1900 - 1960, 58th edition].

Edinburgh, Peebles & Linlithgow Trades' Directory. [1938 - 40th edition; 1960 - 58th edition].

Glasgow and the West of Scotland Carriers Directory. [1900].

Border Counties Trades' Directory. [1960 - 58th edition].

Dumfries, Kirkcudbright & Wigtown Trades' Directory. [1960 - 58th edition].

Dundee & Central Scotland Trades' Directory. [1960 - 58th edition].

Barton's Scottish Trades' Diary. [1903 - 1971].

Glasgow and the west of Scotland Trades Directory. [1903 - 1966].

The Royal National Directory of Scotland. [1903, 1907, 1911].

Munro's Scottish Licensed Trade Directory. [1904 - 1949].

The Court Guide and Royal Blue Book of Scotland. [1905 - 1906].

Scottish Trades & Professional Directory. [1910].

George Souter's Directory for the counties of Inverness, Ross, Caithness and Sutherland. [1920].

Kelly's (Slater's) Directory of Scotland. [1921, 1928].

The Mercantile Directory of Scotland and the North of England. [1922 - 1939].

A New Almanac for the Southern Counties of Scotland: Berwickshire, Roxburghshire, Selkirkshire & Peebleshire. [1922 - 1926].

Angus & Mearns Town & County lists. [1922].

Scottish Press Directory and Advertisers Guide. [1924].

The British Trades Directory. [1924].

Stirling, Linlithgow and Clackmannan Trades' Directory.
[1925 - 1938].

Dumfries, Kirkcudbright and Wigtown Trades' Directory.
[1925 & 1928; 1960 - 58th edition].

Aberdeen, Banff, Kincardine, Moray and Nairn Trades'
Directory, [1928 & 1939].

Murray's Glasgow and West of Scotland Trades Directory.
[1934 & 1936].

ABC General Directory. [1934 - 1936].

Murray's Dundee, Perth and Central Scotland Directory.
[1935 & 1936].

Murray's Edinburgh & South East of Scotland Trades
Directory. [1935 & 1936].

The Trades & Commercial Directory. [1935 & 1936].

Murray's Aberdeen, Inverness and North of Scotland Trades
Directory. [1936].

Edinburgh & South-east Scotland Trades' & Mercantile
Directory. [1938: - established 30 years].

Aberdeen, Inverness and Northern Counties Trades' Directory.
[1938 - 1950].

The Scottish National Register of Classified Trades. [1938
- 1967].

Dumfries, Kirkcudbright and Ayr Trades' Directory. [1943 &
1946].

Western Counties Trades' Directory. [1945 & 1948].

Aberdeen and North of Scotland Trades' Directory. [1947 &
1948, 1960 - 57th edition, 1972].

Stirling, West Lothian and Kinross Trades' Directory.
[1948].

Scotland and Northern Counties Trades' Directory. [1950 -
1953].

Scottish Counties Trades Directory. [1951].

Agricultural Directory of Scotland. [1955].

Northern Counties Register, Edinburgh & Borders Counties
Area. [1963].

Northern Counties Register. Glasgow & the West of Scotland.
[1963].

Chambers Trades Register of Scotland. [1966].

Edinburgh & South-east Scotland Trades' Directory: Berwick, East Lothian, Midlothian, Peebleshire, Roxburghshire, Selkirkshire and West Lothian. [1973].

Thomson Directories. [1981 -]. (For most parts of Scotland, some start a year or two later.)

Catalogue of Directories & poll books in the possession of the Scoiety of Genealogists. [1984].

Directory of Directories: guide to approximately 9600 business & industrial Directories. Cecilia Ann Marlow & Robert C. Thomas. [1987 - 4th ed.].

ABERDEENSHIRE

Aberdeen Almanack. [1774 - 1932].

A Directory for the City of Aberdeen and its Vicinity. [1824 - 1839].

The Aberdeen Almanack and Northern Register. [1816, 1839, 1858, 1867, 1873,1925 - 1932].

The Bon Accord Directory. [1840 - 1845].

The Post Office and Bon Accord Directory. [1846 & 1847].

Post Office Aberdeen Directory. [1848 - 1982].

Cornwall's New Aberdeen Directory. [1853].

Directory of the City of Aberdeen. [1854 - 1968].

Aberdeen & North of Scotland Trades' Directory. [1960 - 58th edition].

Northern County Register. Aberdeen & the North of Scotland. [1963].

Peterhead

Peterhead Almanac & Directory. [1853 & 1864].

The Peterhead Alamanac and Buchan Directory. [1864 & 1865].

ANGUS

Hood's Forfarshire Almanac and Official Directory for the Burghs of Dundee, Arbroath, Montrose, Forfar, Brechin, Kirriemuir. [1880 & 1881].

Forfarshire Directory. [1887].

Dundee

The Dundee Register and Directory. [1782 - 1824].

Dundee delineated. [1822]. A. Colville & Alex M. Sandeman

The Dundee Directory. Chalmer's. [1829 - 1856].

The Dundee Directory and General Register. [1834].

The Dundee Post Office Directory. [1845 - 1871].

The Dundee Directory. [1853 - 1974].

Dundee Courier Almanack, Encyclopaedia & Dictionary. [1897].

Glimpses of Old & New Dundee. [1925].

Dundee, Forfar and Perth Trades' Directory. [1938].

The Dundee Register of Trades and Professions. [1950].

Dundee, Angus & Perth Trades' Directory. [1960 - 58th edition].

Arbroath

The Arbroath Year Book and Directory. [1889- 1950].

Brechin

The Brechin Almanac and Directory. [1886 - 1908].

The Brechin Almanac & Local Handbook. [1890 - 1908, & 1940].

Forfar

The Forfar Directory and Year Book. [1885 - 1960].

The Forfar Annual Directory. [1935].

Montrose

The Montrose Year Book and Directory. [1884 - 1979].

AYRSHIRE

Directory for Ayr. [1830 & 1832].

The Ayrshire Directory. [1851].

North Ayrshire Directory. [1935].

Directory for Ayr, Newton, Wallacetown & Troon. [1841 - 1870].

The Post Office Directory for Ayr, Newton and Wallacetown. [1849 - 1858].

7

Post Office General & Trades Directory for Ayr, Newton and Wallacetown. [1873 - 1912].

The Carrick Directory. [1883].

Ayr and District Directory. [1913 - 1949].

Greenock, Paisley, Renfrew & Ayr Trades Directory. [1960 - 58th edition].

Irvine

Post Office General & Trades Directory for Irvine. [1896].

Kilmarnock

Kilmarnock Directory. [1833].

Kilmarnock & Riccarton Directory. [1840].

The Kilmarnock and Riccarton Post Office Directory. [1846 & 1855].

The Kilmarnock Directory. [1851].

Post Office Kilmarnock Directory. [1862 & 1872].

Jonas' Kilmarnock Directory. [1879].

Kilmarnock Post Office Directory. [1872 - 1913].

Kilmarnock & District Directory. [1923 - 1939].

The Kilmarnock Household, Street & Business Directory. [1957].

BANFFSHIRE

Banffshire Year Book and County Directory. [1875 - 1919].

BERWICKSHIRE

The Berwickshire Family Almanac & Directory. [1892].

The "Advertiser" directory of Berwickshire. [1940].

BUTE

The West Coast Directory. [1883 - 1888].

Bute County Directory. [1889 - 1935].

CAITHNESS & SUTHERLAND

Caithness & Sutherland Almanac. [1922 - 1933].

CLACKMANNANSHIRE

Lothian's Annual Register for the County of Clackmannan. [1877 - 1887].

The County Register & Business Directory for Clackmannanshire. [1889 - 1912].

Alloa

The Alloa illustrated family almanac, district directory & general register for the county of Clackmannanshire. [1887].

DUMBARTONSHIRE

Battrum's Guide & Directory to Helensburgh. [1864, 1869, 1875 - 7th edition].

Macneur & Bryden's Guide & Directory to Helensburgh and its Neighbourhood. [1875 - 1939, 1956].

The Dumbartonshire Directory. [1877 , 1885].

Dumbarton Directory and Almanac. [1892, 1893].

DUMFRIESSHIRE

The County Directory of Dumfriesshire. [1910].

Annan

Guide to Annan & Neighbourhood. [1902].

Annandale Post Office Directory. [1922].

Dumfries

Johnston's Directory of Dumfries & Maxwelltown. [1882].

Post Office Dumfries, Maxwelltown & District Directory. [1893 - 1897].

Dumfries & Maxwelltown Post Office Directory. [1901 & 1903].

Dumfries & District Post Office Directory. [1911 - 1939].

Dumfries & District Directory. [1953 - 1960].

Sanquhar

The Visitors' Guide to Sanquhar & Neighbourhood with a list of people in Business. [1886].

EAST LOTHIAN

The Haddingtonshire Register. [1820 - 1880].

Haddingtonshire Register & Almanac. [1892 - 1918].

The Haddingtonshire Courier Year Book. [1915 - 1960]. Then
The East Lothian Year Book & Guide. [1964 - 1970].

Dunbar

Dunbar Burgh Register & Guide. John Macdonald. [1897].

FIFESHIRE

Fife & Kinross Register. [1814 - 1895].

Westwood's Parochial Directory of Fife & Kinross. [1862 & 1866].

The Fife News illustrated Almanac. [1895, 1900, 1905,].

The Fife News & Coast Chronicle illustrated Almanac. [1912, 1914, 1916].

The Fife News Almanac. [1915, 1923, 1932].

The Tayside Annual and Directory for Newport, Wormit and Tayport. [1907 & 1908].

Fife & Kinross Trades' Directory, (including Stirling & Clackmannan). [1908 - 1966, (1960 - 59th edition)].

Fife Directory. [1982].

Burntisland

Burntisland Directory & Illustrated year book. [1892].

Dunfermline

The Dunfermline Register. [1829 - 1871].

Directory for the Town of Dunfermline. [1832, 1834].

The Dunfermline Almanac & Register. [1835].

The Dunfermline Directory. [1890 - 1898].

The Directory of Dunfermline, Inverkeithing, and Naval Base (including Townhill & Kingseat). [1909 - 1912].

Dunfermline Trades' & Professions Directory. [1967].

Kirkcaldy

Thomson's Directory for Kirkcaldy. [1834, 1835].

The Kirkcaldy Directory. [1882 - 1936].

Kirkcaldy & Dysart Directory. [1924].

St. Andrews

St. Andrews Directory. [1935].

INVERNESSHIRE

Inverness County Directory. [1887 - 1920].

Inverness

The Inverness Directory. [1873, 1970].

Inverness Burgh Directory. [1866 - 1960].

KIRKCUDBRIGHTSHIRE

Stewartry of Kirkcudbright Post Office Directory. [1921 & 1924].

LANARKSHIRE

Upper Ward of Lanarkshire Almanac & handbook. [1860 - 1902]

The Lanarkshire Business Directory. [1895].

Glasgow & Lanark trades Directory. [1901 - 1960, 58th edition].

Glasgow Trades Directory including Lanarkshire. [1905 - 1928].

Airdrie

Clarke's Airdrie Directory. [1896].

Glasgow

Glasgow Almanack. [1763 - 1806].

Glasgow Register. J. Bryce. [1781].

John Tait's Directory for the City of Glasgow. [1783. reprinted 1871].

Post Office Glasgow Directory. [1783 - 1978].

Jones' Directory or useful pocket companion for the City of Glasgow. [1787 - reprint 1868; 1789 - reprint 1866; 1790].

McFeat's Glasgow Directory. [1804 - 1828].

Topographical Picture of Glasgow in its ancient & modern state. [1820 - 3rd edition]. R. Chapman.

Jamaica Street & round about it in the year 1820 by a burgess of Glasgow. Glasgow, Lindsay, 1891.

Glasgow delineated; or a description of that city, its institutions, manufacturers and Commerce. [1821, 1824, 1826, 1836].

11

Description of Glasgow. J. Cleland. [1840].

Glasgow Commercial List. [1869 - 1870] with Greenock
    [1870 - 1872], with Edinbrugh & Leith   [1873 -
    1874]. Then Scottish Commercial List [1876 - 1900].

Slater's Royal National Commercial Directory of Glasgow.
    [1880].

The National Telephone Company Glasgow District List of
    Subscribers, issue 16. [1886].

Glasgow of today. The metropolis of the North. Businessmen &
    mercantile interests. [1886].

Glasgow today & manual of commerce, historical, statistical
    & biographical. [1888].

Russell's Glasgow & Suburban Street Guide. [1890].

Adshead's Penny Street Directory of Greater Glasgow.   [1892
    - 1936].

J. McCormick & Son, Glasgow Trades' Directory.   [1905 -
    1923].

Kelly's Directory for Glasgow. [1923 - 1974].

Glasgow Post Office Telephone Directory. [1929 - 1932].

Glasgow Royal Exchange Directory of Members, Firms & Trades.
    [1933 & 1934].

J.S. Clarke's Evening News Encyclopaedia of Glasgow. nos. 1
    - 300. [1935 - 1936].

J.H. Tierney's Early Glasgow Newspapers, periodicals and
    directories. [1934].

V.P. Street Directory of Greater Glasgow. [1948].

Glasgow Area Classified Telephone Directory, Trades' &
    Professions. [1949].

Chamber's Trades Register of Glasgow & District.   [1957 -
    1959].

Chamber's Trades Register of Glasgow & Clydeside. [1960].

Hamilton

The Hamilton Directory. [1847].

Brown's Hamilton Directory. [1855].

Hamilton Directory. [1859 & 1878].

Handbook of Hamilton, Bothwell, Blantyre and Uddingston with
    a Directory. [1862].

The Hamilton Directory. [1883 & 1889].

Peat & Forrest's Directory of Hamilton, Blantyre & Larkhall.
[1884].

Directory for Hamilton and district including Cadzow,
Eddlewood, Ferniegair, Larkhall, High Blantyre and
Bothwell. [1909].

Motherwell

History & Directory of Motherwell. [1894 & 1899].

Clarke's Motherwell Directory. [1896].

Directory for Motherwell and District. [1910].

Motherwell & Wishaw Directory. [1957].

Uddingston

Uddingston Directory. [1887 - 1899].

Wishaw

Pomphrey's Directory & Handbook of Wishaw with Shotts
Supplement. [1887 & 1893].

Directory for Wishaw and District. [1909].

MIDLOTHIAN

A Companion to Captain Armstrong & Son's Map of the Three
Lothians, Towns, Villages, Seats, etc.. [1773].

The Edinburgh County Directory. [1870].

Dalkeith

Dalkeith Directory & Almanac. [1878, 1885].

Carment's Directory for Dalkeith & District. [1887 - 1917]

Dalkeith & District Directory & Household Almanac. [1890 &
1894].

Edinburgh

List of owners of property in Edinburgh, 1635. C.B. Boog
Watson, B.O.T.O.E.C., vol.13, 1924.

Ane list of the neighbours & Inhabitants within the Town of
Edinburgh truely given up by the respective constables
therein as follows taken in May 1682. Bound with the
same for Canongate, North Leith & South Leith, May
1682. [86 pp. Ms. Central Lib. Edinburgh].

The Edinburgh Almanack. [1738 - 1836]. Then: Oliver &
Boyd's New Edinburgh Almanac. [1837 - 1886]. Then:
Oliver & Boyd's New Edinburgh Almanac & National
Repository. [1887 - 1932].

A Directory of Edinburgh in 1752. Compiled by J. Gilhooley
    Edinburgh, 1988.

Williamson's Directory for the city of Edinburgh, Canongate,
    Leith & Suburbs. [1773 - 1796].

The Edinburgh Directory. (Aitchison's). [1793 - 1803].

Denovan & Co's Edinburgh Directory. [1804].

Post Office Edinburgh & Leith Directory. [1805 - 1974].

The New & Improved Directory for Edinburgh, Leith & Suburbs.
    [1824].

John Veitch.   A curious & humerous arrangement of surnames,
    containing about 800 living characters in the   City   of
    Edinburgh, with professions & additions. [1825].

John Veitch's, The Novel Directory. [1825, 1826, 1827].

Gray's Annual   Directory of Edinburgh & Vicinity.   [1832 -
    1838].

The New Edinburgh, Leith & County (business) Directory.
    [1867 & 1870].

The   New   Edinburgh,   Leith & County Household Directory.
    [1868].

The Edinburgh Directory. [1870].

Parochial Directory for Edinburgh & Leith. [1888 & 1893].

Municipal & parochial Directory & voters'   guide   for
    Edinburgh & Leith. [1892].

McLaren's Edinburgh & Leith Street Directory. [1902 &
    1902].

The   National   Telephone Company's   Special   Supplemental
    Directory for Edinburgh & Leith. [1903].

List of Subscribers for Edinburgh District.   Post Office
    Telephone Service. [1916].

Edinburgh,   Peebles and Linlithgow   Trades'   Directory.
    [1940].

Edinburgh Area Classified Telephone Directory, Trades &
    Professions. [1950].

Thomson Directory Edinburgh & Surrounding Area. [1982 -   ].

Musselburgh

Musselburgh Directory & Year Book. [1903].

Musselburgh Directory. [1934 & 1937].

Portobello

Portobello Pocket Directory. [1836 - 1837].

The Portobello & District Directory. [1889 - 1914].

MORAYSHIRE

Russell's Morayshire Register & Elgin & Forres Directory. [1844, 1847, 1850, 1852].

Black's Morayshire Directory (including upper part of Banffshire). [1863].

Moray & Nairn Directory. [1888 - 1889].

Grantown

The Grantown Almanack. [1907].

ORKNEY & SHETLAND

Zetland Directory & Guide. [1861 - 2nd edition].

Peace's Orkney Almanac & County Directory. [1861 - 1939].

The Orkney & Shetland Guide Directory & Almanac, [1882 - 1893].

Manson's Shetland Almanac & Directory. [1892 - 1950].

PERTHSHIRE

Leslie's Directory for Perth & Perthshire. [1885 - 1939].

Morison's Perthshire Register & City of Perth Directory. [1886 & 1887].

Perthshire Directory. [1889].

Perth Town & County Directory. [1948].

Alyth

Lunan's Alyth Almanac & List of Voters. [1888].

McMurray's Alyth Directory & Almanac. [1911 & 1913].

Coupar Angus

Stewart's Coupar Angus & District Directory & Almanac. [1905].

Perth

Directory for the City of Perth & Vicinity. [1837 & 1841].

The Post Office Perth Directory. [1843 - 1884].

The Annual Directory for the City of Perth. [1890].

RENFREWSHIRE

Fowler's Commercial Directory of the Principal Towns & Villages in the Upper Ward of Renfrewshire. [1829 - 1836].

Fowler's Commercial Directory of the lower Ward of Renfrewshire. [1831 - 1836].

Greenock, Paisley, Renfrewshire & Ayr Trades' Directory. [1960 - 58th edition].

Barrhead

Clarke's Barrhead & Neilston Directory. [1896].

Gourock

The Gourock Directory. [1925 & 1935].

Greenock

Greenock & Port Glasgow Directory. [1805].

Hutcheson's Greenock Register, Directory & General Advertiser. [1841 & 1845].

The Post Office Greenock Directory. [1847 - 1915].

The Handbook for the Burgh of Greenock. [1923 & 1926].

The Greenock Directory. [1923 - 1957].

Kemp's Greenock & District Local Directory. [1966].

Paisley

The Paisley Directory. [1810 - 1828].

Fowler's Paisley Commercial Directory. [1838 - 1853].

The Paisley New Directory. [1840].

Paisley's Commercial Directory. [1844].

Sproull's Paisley Commercial Directory. [1848].

Hinshelwood's Directory for Paisley & Neighbourhood. [1857 - 1861].

Watson's Directory for Paisley, Renfrew, Johnstone, Elderslie, Linwood, Quarrelton, Thornhill, Balaclava & Inkerman. [1862 - 1883].

Winning's Paisley Directory & General Advertiser. [1864 & 1866].

The Paisley Directory & General Advertiser. [1884 - 1937]

The Paisley Household Almanack. [1889].

Kilmalcolm

Kilmalcolm Directory. [1906].

ROXBURGHSHIRE

Rutherford's Household Almanac & yearbook of useful knowledge, especially for Roxburghshire. [1862 - 1864].

SELKIRKSHIRE

The Galashiels & Selkirk Almanac & Directory. [1889 - 1903]. Then ......

Galashiels, Selkirk & Melrose Almanac & Directory. [1912 - 1961].

STIRLINGSHIRE

The Stirlingshire [Burgh & County] Directory. [1886].

Threepenny Guide & Directory for Stirling, Bridge of Allan, Dunblane, Doune, St. Ninians & Bannockburn. [1886].

Falkirk

Falkirk & District Illustrated Almanac, Diary & Directory. [1913].

Falkirk, Grangemouth & District Directory. [1934].

Falkirk Directory & Guide. [1955].

Grangemouth

The Grangemouth Directory & Guide. [1949, 1955, 1963].

Stirling

The Stirling Directory including Bridge of Allan, St. Ninians, Cambusbarron, Whins of Milton & Bannockburn. [1870].

The Stirling Directory. [1872 - 1888].

Wilson's Business Directory of Stirling, Bridge of Allan, Causewayhead, Bannockburn & Neighbourhood. [1887 & 1888].

Harvey's Stirling Directory & Almanac. [1888 - 1894].

Cook & Wylie's Stirling Directory & Almanac. [1896 - 1909].

Industries of Stirling & District. [1909].

Scott, Learmonth & Allan's Directory for Stirling. [1913].

Stirling District Directory. [1913 - 1932].

Stirling & District Directory [official]. [1925].

WEST LOTHIAN

Courier Yearbook & Directory for Broxburn & Uphall.[1909].

Brown's Almanac. [West, Mid, east Calder, Fauldhouse & East
    Mid Lothian]. [1909].

West Lothian District Council: Business Directories.   [1988
    -      ].

INDIA

[see under respective trades also]

General

East India Register. [1803 - 1842]. Then:

Asiatic Journal & Monthly Register for British India. [1816 - 1845].

India Register. [1843 - 1860]. Then:

Indian Army & Civil Service List. [1862 - 1876].

India List. [1877 - 1895].

India Office List. [1886 - 1895]. Then:

India List & India Office List. [1896 - 1906]. Then:

India Office List. [1907 - 1937]. Then:

India Office List & Burma Office List. [1938 - 1947].

Bengal

Bengal Directory. [1815 - 1823].

Bengal Directory & General Register. [1824 - 1845].

Calcutta kalendar. [1821].

Calcutta annual Register & Directory. [1814 - 1835].

New Calcutta Directory. [1856 - 1862]

Thacker's Bengal Directory. [1863 - 1884]. Then:

Thacker's Indian Directory. [1886 - 1960].

East India Company's Bengal Civil Servants, 1780 - 1838. Edward Dodwell & James Samuel Miles.

Bombay

Bombay Kalendar & Register. [1806 - 1828]. Then:

Bombay Calendar & Almanac. [1829 - 1844]. Then:

Bombay Calendar. [1845] Then:

Bombay Calendar & General Directory. [1846 - 1851]. Then:

Bombay Almanac & Directory. [1851 - 1868].

East India Company's Bombay Civil Servants, 1798 - 1839. Edward Dodwell & James Samuel Miles.

19

Madras

Madras Almanac. [1800 - 1861]. Then:

Asylum Press Almanac. [1862 - 1936].

East India Company's Madras Civil Servants, 1780 - 1839. Edward Dodwell & James Samuel Miles.

Records of Services of the Honourable East India Company's Civil Servants in the Madras Presidency, from 1741 - 1858. Charles Campbell Prinsep, 1885.

Military

Indian Army List. [1891 - 1946].

East India Company's Military Oficers. [1788 - 1792].

Officers of the Indian Army Reserve of Officers. [1916 - 1918].

List of the Officers of the Bengal Army, 1758 - 1834. Vernon Charles Paget Hodson, 1927 - 1947.

ACTUARIES

The History of the Faculty of Actuaries in Scotland, 1856-1956. Andrew Rutherford Davidson, Edinburgh, 1956.

AGRICULTURE

General view of the Agriculture:

of the county of Angus or Forfar. Rev. Rodger, Edinburgh, 1794.

of the county of Argyll. J. Smith, 1798.

of the county of Argyll & the western part of Inverness-shire. J. Robson, 1794.

of the county of Berwick. R. Kerr, 1809.

of the county of Clydesdale. John Naismith, Brentford, 1794.

in the county of Dumbarton. David Ure, London, 1794.

of the county of Dumfries. Bryce Johnston, London, 1794.

and rural economy of East Lothian. George Buchanan Hepburn, Edinburgh, 1794.

of the county of Fife. J. Thomson, 1800.

of Galloway. S. Smith, 1810.

of the Hebrides. J. Macdonald, 1810.

of the county of Kincardine. George Robertson, 1813.

of the county of Mid-Lothian. George Robertson, Edinburgh, 1795.

of the county of Moray, lying between the Spey & Findhorn. James Donaldson, London, 1794.

of the county of Nairn the eastern coast of Inverness-shire. James Donaldson, London, 1794.

of the county of Peebles. Rev. Charles Findlater, 1802.

of the county of Perth. J. Robertson, Perth, 1799.

in the southern districts of Perth. James Robertson, London, 1794.

of the county of Renfrew. John Wilson, Paisley, 1812.

of the county of Roxburgh. David Ure, London, 1794.

of the county of Selkirk. Thomas Johnston, London, 1794.

of the county of Tweedale. Thomas Johnston, London, 1794.

of the county of West Lothian. James Trotter, Edinburgh, 1794.

APPRENTICES

General

Patterns of migration of apprentices into Aberdeen & Inverness during the 18th & early 19th centuries. Ian D. Whyte, Scott. Geogr. Mag. vol. 102 Sept. 1986.

Aberdeen

Register of Indentures of the burgh of Aberdeen, 1622 - 1878. Scottish Notes & Queries, x, xi, xii.

Edinburgh

Register of Edinburgh Apprentices, 1583-1800. Ed. Francis J. Grant, Marguerite Wood. Scott. Rec. Soc., 3vols., 1906-1963.

ARCHERS

The History of the Royal Company of Archers, 1951-1976. Sir Alastair Blair, Edinburgh, 1977.

The History of the Royal Company of Archers. J.B. Paul, Edinburgh, 1875.

The Royal Company of Archers. Joyce Dunford, in Scott. Field, vol.123, 1976.

The Royal Company of Archers 1675 - 1951. Ian Hay, Edinburgh, 1951.

Bowmen body guard of Scotland. Nigel Tranter, in Country Life, vol. 160, 1976.

The Royal Company of Archers, List of Members 1st November, 1903.

ARCHITECTS

General

A Biographical Dictionary of British Architects, 1600 - 1840. Howard Colvin, revised edition 1978, London.

Architects of the Highlands in the 19th Century: a sketch. John Gifford, in Bull. Scot. Georgian Soc., no.7, 1980.

Scottish Architects at Home & Abroad. Exhib. Cat., T.A. Cherry & I.G. Brown, Edinburgh, 1978.

Blower's Architect's, Surveyor's, Engineer's & Builder's Directory. [1860].

The Architects', Engineers' & Building Trades' Directory. [1868].

Directory of Architects', Builders' and of Importers & users of building materials. William Bridges, 1905.

Architects' & Surveyors' Directory & Referendum. [1907 –
     1912].

Who's Who in Architecture. [1914, 1923, 1926].

Dundee

Architects & Architecture in Dundee, 1770 – 1914. David M.
     Walker, Abertay Historical Society, no.18, 1977.

ARMS & ARMS MAKERS

Scottish Arms Makers.   C.E.Whitelaw, ed. Sarah Barter,
     London, 1977.

Scottish Firearms. W.   Reid,   in Pollard's history of
     firearms, Feltham, 1983.

The Scottish Armoury. David H. Caldwell, Edinburgh, 1979.

European hand firearms of the 16th, 17th & 18th centuries.
     With a treatise on Scottish hand firearms. Herbert J.
     Jackson, 1923.

Pistols

The Book of guns & gunsmiths. Anthony North & Ian V. Hogg,
     Glasgow, 1977.

Scottish Pistols. Hamish Sloan & James B. McKay,   in
     Dispatch, nos.99–106, 1982–1984.

Scottish Pistols: a Celtic Style. David H. Caldwell,   in
     Dispatch, no.103, 1983.

Doune

The Pistol Makers of Doune. A.C. McKerracher, in Country
     Life, vol.167, 1980.

Swords

Glasgow or Stirling. Colin Roland, in Dispatch, no.104,
     1983.

Early Scottish Basket-hilted Swords, c.1600-1700. Anthony D.
     Darling, in Dispatch, no. 109, 1985.

ARTISTS

Galleries & other collections

Most galleries keep detailed records of their holdings
and are willing to let the serious student have access to
their records. Some compile biographical notes on artists
and keep details of other pictures not in their collection.
However, it most cases it is necessary to make   an

appointment, as few galleries will entertain a casual visitor. Quite often a letter will elicit the information required.

There are too many galleries to list here. The most useful are:

The Scottish National Portrait Gallery, Queen Street, Edinburgh, EH2

The National Portrait Gallery, St. Martin's Place, London, WC2H 0HE

The Victoria & Albert Museum, Cromwell Road, London, SW7 2RL

There are also two centres which collect photographs of portraits and paintings and have them arranged by artist. In both cases an appointment is unecessary. They are:

University of London, Courtauld Institute of Art, 20 Portman Square, London, W1H 0BE

The Paul Mellon Centre for Studies in British Art, 20 Bloomsbury Square, London WC1A 2NS

The Scottish Record Office, Register House, Edinburgh, EH1 3YY, has compiled a card index of references to artists contained in the Gifts and Deposits section. These cards may contain much useful information as to sitter, price, transportation of works, etc..

Some specialist art libraries have compiled very useful catalogues of articles and books about individual artists. They are often on cards or paper slips and are arranged alphabetically by artist. One such collection is kept by: Edinburgh Central Library, George IV Bridge, Edinburgh EH1 1EG.

Dictionaries

Dictionaries of artists tend to give brief details: name, dates, country, representative price, major works, but the more specialised the dictionary the more information there is. Although some are in a foreign language it is comparitively easy to extract the main information.

A Book of Sporting Painters. London, 1931. W.S.Sparrow

A Concise Dictionary of Scottish Painters. Paul Harris, Edinburgh, 1977.

Angling in British Art. London, 1923. W.S.Sparrow.

Artists' Directory. [1874].

British Nineteenth Century Marine Painting, 1974 Antique Collectors' Club. Denys Brook-Hart.

British Silhouette Artists & their work, 1760 - 1860. Sue McKechnie, London, 1978.

British Sporting Artists. London, 1922. W.S.Sparrow.

British Twentieth Century Marine Painting, 1981 Antique Collectors' Club. Denys Brook-Hart

Bryan's Dictionary of Painters & Engravers, London 1903, 5 vols.

Classified Directory of Artists' Signatures, Symbols & Monograms. 1983 P. Grahame Publishing. H.H.Caplan

Dictionaires de Peintures, Sculpteurs, Dessinateurs et Graveurs. Paris, 1976, 10 vols. E. Benezit

Dictionary of British Animal Painters. 1973, F. Lewis Pubn. Lt. Col. J.C.Wood.

Dictionary of British Artists 1880 - 1940. 1988, ed. J.Johnson and A.Greutzner.

Dictionary of British Bird Painters, 1974. Frank Lewis.

Dictionary of British Book Illustrators - The Twentieth Century, London 1983. Brigid Peppin & Lucy Mickelthwait.

Dictionary of British Book Illustrators & Caricaturists, 1800-1914. Suffolk, 1978. Simon Houfe.

Dictionary of British Equestrian Artists. Antique Collectors' Club 1985, Sally Mitchell.

Dictionary of British Etchers. Col. Maurice Harold Grant.

Dictionary of British Flower, Fruit & Still Life Painters. 1974, 2 vols. F.Lewis Pubn. R. Brinsley Burbidge.

Dictionary of British Landscape Painters, Sixteenth to Twentieth Century, 1952, F.Lewis publication. Col. Maurice Harold Grant.

Dictionary of British Medallists. Col. Maurice Harold Grant.

Dictionary of British Narrative Painters. 1978, F. Lewis Pubn. Stephen Sartin

Dictionary of British Portraiture. Batsford, 1979-1981, 4 vols.

Dictionary of British Sporting Painters. 1965 F. Lewis Pubn. Sydney Herbert Pavière.

Dictionary of British Water-colour Artists up to 1920. 1976 2 vols., Antique Collectors Club. H.L.Mallalieu.

Dictionary of Water-colour Painters 1750-1900. 1972 Stanley W. Fisher F.R.S.A..

Dictionary of Irish Artists. Dublin 1913, 2 vols. reprinted 1989.W.G.Strickland

Dictionary of Victorian Landscape Painters. 1968, F. Lewis Pubn.. Sydney Herbert Pavière.

Dictionary of Victorian Painters, 1978. C. Wood

Künstler Lexikon. Leipzig, 1907. 37 vols. + 8 supplementary
vols. U. Thieme & F. Becker.

Mongrams of Victorian & Edwardian Artists. 1976, Victoria
Square Press. Peter Nahum.

Painters in Scotland 1301-1700. Scottish Record Society,
1978. M.R.Apted & S.Hannabuss.

Who's Who in Art, 1927 -   , 23 vols.

Engravers & Sitters

Before the advent of photography, engravings and mezzotints
were the main vehicle by which likenesses of people received
a wider audience. There are not many general works, but
those that do exist usually contain information about the
sitter as well as the engraver.

British Mezzotints Portraits. London 1882-1884. John
Chaloner Smith.

British Prints. A Dictionary & price guide, 1987, Antique
Collectors Club. Ian Mackenzie.

Catalogue of Drawings by British Artists. 4 vols. British
Museum, 1898 Laurence Binyon.

Catalogue of Engraved British Portraits, 6 vols. 1908+ ,
British Museum. ed. Freeman O'Donoghue F.S.A.

Edinburgh Engravers. Book of the Old Edinburgh Club, vol. 9,
1916. John C. Guy.

Original Portraits. 4 Vols. 1837 Edinburgh. John Kay

Scottish Engravers to c. 1820. O.U.P. 1949. George Herbert
Bushnell.

Sporting Aquatints & their Engravers 1775-1820. F.Lewis
Pubn. 1978. Charles Lane.

Exhibitors & Exhibitions

Although there are too many exhibitions to list, some of the
larger Societies have produced compilations of their annual
exhibitions. Once again these works may give information
about the sitter as well.

Royal Academy Exhibitors 1769-1904. 8 vols. London
1905-1906. Algernon Graves

Royal Academy Exhibitors 1905-1970. 6 vols. E.P.Publishing
1973+.

Royal Hibernian Academy of Arts. Index of Exhibitors
1826-1979, 3 vols. ed. Ann M. Stewart

Royal Scottish Academy 1826-1916. Academicians & exhibits. Glasgow 1917. W.D.McKay

Royal Scottish Academy, [History of] 1826-1976. Esme Gordon.

Royal Society of British Artists Exhibitors 1824-1962. 5 Vols. F.Lewis Pubn. 1973-1977. Maurice Bradshaw

Royal Society of British Artists 1824-1893 & New English Art Club 1888-1917. Antique Collectors Club 1975. Compiled by Jane Johnson.

Society of Artists 1760-1791 & the Free Art Society 1761-1783. London 1907. Algernon Graves F.S.A.

Walpole Society Vol. 27, 1938/1939 by Hugh Gatty. This work gives additional information about sitters in portraits exhibited at the Society of Artists & The Free Society of Artists, as recorded by Horace Walpole, 1760 - 1791.

Works Exhibited at the Royal Society of British Artists 1824 - 1893: and the New English Art Club, 2 vols.. The Antique Collectors Club, 1975.

Miniaturists & Miniatures

Miniatures were used in place of photographs by the more well-to-do, and sitters names are given where known.

Collecting Miniatures. Antique Collectors Club 1979. Daphne Foskett.

Dictionary of British Miniature Painters. 2 Vols. Faber & Faber 1972. Daphne Foskett.

Miniatures - a Dictionary & Guide. Antique Collectors Club 1987. Daphne Foskett.

Miniature Painters - British & Foreign. 2 vols. London 1903. J.J.Foster.

Portraits & Sitters

Several compilations of portraits have been published, including those in the Royal Collection. These tend to be of the more famous or wealthy people of history, but often only a description of the work is provided with a few representative illustrations. However, notes are usually given as to the location of the paintings and in some cases one can get to view them. Black & White photographs may be available from the Witt Library & Paul Mellon Centre [see above].
Many works on stately homes contain references to and reproductions of portraits in their collections, but are too numerous to mention.

The Portrait Gallery of Distinguished Females, including beauties of the courts of George IV & William IV. John Burke, 2 vols., 1833.

Early Victorian Portraits, 2 vols. 1973 H.M.S.O.. Richard
   Ormrod.

Early Georgian Portraits, 2 vols. H.M.S.O. 1977. John
   Kerslake.

Later Georgian Pictures in the Royal Collection, 2 vols.
   Phaidon 1969 Oliver Millar.

National Portrait Gallery Complete Illustrated Catalogue.
   N.P.G. 1981. Compiled by K.K.Young.

A survey of Portraits in Welsh Houses. 2 vols. 1957,
   Cardiff. John H. Steegman.

Regency Portraits, 2 vols. N.P.G. 1985. Richard Walker.

Tudor & Jacobean Portraits, 2 vols. H.M.S.O. 1979. Roy
   Strong.

Tudor, Stuart & Early Georgian Pictures in the Royal
   Collection, 2 vols. Phaidon 1963. Oliver Millar.

Women Artists

Not a great deal of work has been done on women artists in
the past, but the number of works available is growing.

The Obstacle Race, London 1979. Germaine Greer.

Victorian Women Artists. Women's Press, London 1987. Pamela
   Gerrish Nunn.

Women & Art. London 1978. Elsa Honig Fine.

Women Artists. Women's Press, London 1978. Karen Petersen &
   J.J.Wilson.

Women Painters of the World. London, 1905. W.S.Sparrow

Sculptors

Bronze Sculptors & Founders, 1800-1930. 4 vols. Chicago
   1974-1980. Harold Berman.

Dictionary of British Sculptors, 1660-1851. London 1968.
   Rupert Gunnis.

Dictionary of British Sculptors. London 1953. Col. Maurice
   Harold Grant.

New Dictionary of Modern Sculpture. New York 1970. ed.
   Robert Mailhard.

SCOTLAND

Art as a family affair the Fraser brothers. Charles Lane, in
   Country Life, vol.165, 1979.

Stirlingshire

The artists of Craigmill & Cambuskenneth, 1880-1920
   :[catalogue]. Fiona Wilson, Stirling, 1978.

AUCTIONEERS

The Auctioneers', Land Agents' Valuers', & Estate Agents'
   Directory. [1860, 1862].

A Diary & Directory for the use of Surveyors, Auctioneers,
   Land & Estate Agnets. [1888 - 1939].

AUTHORS

Some old Scottish authors whose books were printed abroad.
   David Murray, Trans. Glasgow Archaeol. Soc., Glasgow,
   1921.

Scottish Men of Letters in the 18th Century. Henry Grey
   Graham, London, 1901.

Authors' & Writers' Who's Who. [1934 - 1963].

The Bookman Directory of Booksellers, Publishers & Authors.
   [1893].

BAKERS

Scottish Bakers' year book. J.H. Adam, Leith, 1896.

Glasgow

The Corporation of Bakers, Glasgow. James B. Tennent,
   Glasgow, 1899.

The Bakers' Incorporation of Glasgow. J. Ness, Glasgow,
   1891.

The Incorporation of Bakers of Glasgow. Glasgow 1931. 3rd
   edition, 1948.

St. Andrews

The Baxter books of St. Andrews, a record of three
   centuries. J.H. Macadam, Scot. Assoc. of Bakers.
   Edinburgh, 1902.

Stirling

The Incorporation of Bakers of Stirling. David B. Morris,
   Stirling, 1923.

BANDS

Society of trained Bands of Edinburgh, 1663 - 1874. ed
   William Skinner, 1889.

BANKS AND BANKING

General

Scottish Banking, 1695-1973. S.G. Checkland, Glasgow, 1975.

The Royal Bank of Scotland, 1727-1977. Edinburgh 1977.

History of the Royal Bank of Scotland, 1727-1927. Neil Munro, Edinburgh 1928.

The Bank of Scotland, 1695-1945. Charles A. Malcolm, Edinburgh, n.d..

Our Bank. [The Commercial Bank of Scotland Ltd. 1810-1946] 2nd ed. 1946, Edinburgh.

The National Bank of Scotland Centenary, 1825-1925. Edinburgh, 1925.

The National Bank of Scotland Ltd.. Edinburgh, 1948.

The British Linen Bank, 1746-1946. Charles A. Malcolm, Edinburgh, 1950.

The Life Cycle of the Union Bank of Scotland, 1830-1954. Norio Tamaki, Aberdeen, 1983.

The Scottish Provincial Banking Companies, 1747-1864. Charles W. Munn, Edinburgh, 1981. [This has an excellent bibliography and reference section on Scottish Banking].

Some Scottish Banking Families. J.M. Kennedy, Scottish Genealogist, vols. 6 & 7.

Dundee

A century of Banking in Dundee: 1764-1864. C.W. Boase, 2nd. ed., Edinburgh, 1867.

Glasgow

The Savings Bank of Glasgow. J.D.Campbell, c.1986.

Perth

A brief sketch of the History, Aims and Practices of the Savings Bank of the county and city of Perth Centenary 1815-1915. Perth, 1915.

BARBERS

Edinburgh

The Princes Street Proprietors. [contains Barbers of Edinburgh & the Canongate]. David Robertson, Edinburgh, 1935.

Glasgow

Records of the Incorporation of Barbers of Glasgow.
formerly chirugeons and barbers]. J.B. Tennant,
Glasgow, 1899.

History & Records of the Incorporation of Barbers in
Glasgow. F.S. Batchelor, Glasgow, 1979.

BIRTH-BRIEVES

Birth brieves from the registers of the burgh of Aberdeen,
1635-1805. J. Stuart, Miscellany of the Old Spalding
Club, vol.5, Aberdeen, 1852.

BLACKSMITHS

Scottish stone cutters & blacksmiths who came to Texas 1880.
Robert W. Baumgardner, Aberdeen & N.E. Scotland F.H.S.
Journal, no.22, 1987.

BONNET MAKERS & DYERS

History of the Incorporation of Bonnet-makers & Dyers of
Glasgow, 1597-1950. Mathew Lindsay, Glasgow, 1952.

The Hatters' Gazette Diary and Trade Directory. [1925 -
1948].

BREWERS & BREWING

Scottish Brewery Trade Marks.[1876-1900]. Edward Burns,
Glasgow, c.1986.

Scottish Brewery Trade Marks, 1900 - 1976. Edward Burns,
Glasgow, 1987.

Sources of capital & capitalization in the Scottish Brewing
Industry, c.1750-1830.

The Whiskey Distillers of the U.K.. Alfred Barnard, Devon,
1969.

A History of the Brewing Industry in Scotland. Ian
Donnachie, Edinburgh, 1979.

Kelly's Directory of the Wine & Spirits Trades, Brewers &
Maltsters. [1877 - 1939].

Trades' Directory to the Brewers, Corn, Seed, Provision &
Wine & Spirit Trades. [1894].

The Incorporated Brewers' Directory. [1927 - 1950].

Alloa

Alloa Ale: a history of the brewing industry in Alloa.
Charles McMaster, Edinburgh 1985?

Edinburgh

The Fellowship & Society of Brewers of Ale & Beer in Edinburgh. B.O.T.O.E.C., vol.10, 1924.

The petition of the several Brewars in and about Edinburgh under subscribing. July 29th, 1725. [pamphlet] Edinburgh, 1725.

Glasgow

Chronicles and history of the Maltman Craft or Incorporation of Glasgow, 1605-1879. R. Douie, Glasgow, 1879; revised by F.G. Dougall to 1895, Glasgow, 1895.

BRICK-MAKERS

A Survey of Scottish brickmarks. G.J.Douglas, Glasgow, 1985. In Scottish Industrial Archaeology Survey.

BRUSHMAKERS

Directory of the brush and allied trades. [1948 - 1967].

BURGESSES, ALDERMEN AND GUILD BRETHEREN

Aberdeen

Memorials of the Aldermen, Provosts and Lord Provosts of Aberdeen. A.M.Munro, 1895.

List of the Deans of Guild of Aberdeen. A. Walker, 1875

Register of Burgesses of the Burgh of Aberdeen, 1399-1700. New Spalding Club Miscellany, vols. 1 & 2, 1890, & 1908 ed. by Alexander M. Munro.

Merchant and Craft guilds. E. Bain, Aberdeen, 1889.

Ayr

Proceedings of the Gild Court of Ayr. T. Dickson, Ayr & Wigtown Arch. Assoc. vol.1, Edinburgh, 1878.

Dumbarton

Roll of Dumbarton Burgess & Guild Bretheren, 1600-1846. Fergus Roberts, Scottish Record Society, 1937.

Dundee

The Roll of Eminent Burgesses of Dundee, 1513-1887. A.H. Millar, Dundee, 1887.

Dunfermline

The Guild Court Book of Dunfermline, 1433-1597. Ed. Elizabeth P.D.Torrie. Scottish Record Society, 1986.

Edinburgh

The Guildry of Edinburgh. James Colston, Edinburgh, 1887.

The Incorporated Trades of Edinburgh. James Colston, Edinburgh, 1891. [Chirugeons, Hammermen, Goldsmiths, Baxters, Fleschouris, Mary's Chapel, Skinners & Furriers, Cordwainers, Talzouris, Wobstaris, Waekaris, Bonnet makers, Candlemakers, Barbers.]

Edinburgh Guilds & Crafts. Sir James D. Marwick, Edinburgh, 1909.

History of the Edinburgh Chamber of Commerce and Manufacturers, from 1785-1861. Sir George Harrison.

Roll of Edinburgh Burgesses & Guild Bretheren, 1406-1841, 3vols. C.B.Boog Watson, Scottish Record Society, 1929-1933.

List of the Deans of Guild of the city of Edinburgh, 1403-1890. T.G. Stevenson, Edinburgh, 1890.

Glasgow

The Burgesses & Guild Bretheren of Glasgow, 1573-1846, 2vols. James R. Anderson, Scottish Record Society, 1925 & 1931.

Kelso

Ancient & Modern: a history of the incorporated trades, guilds & commerce of Kelso. J.L.Trainer, Kelso, 1990.

Perth

Guild acts or laws for the Guildrie incorporation Perth, 1670-1911. John Thomas, Perth, 1911.

Stirling

The Stirling Guildry Book, 1592-1846. W.B. Cook, Glasg. Stirligsh. and Sons of the Rock Soc., Glasgow, 1916.

Extracts from the records of the merchant guild of Stirling, 1592-1846. W.B. Cook & David B. Morris, Stirling, 1916.

CABINET MAKERS

General

Georgian Cabinet Makers. Ralph Edwards & Margaret Jourdain, revised edition 1955.

The Chairs of Sutherland & Caithness. R. Ross Noble, in Reg. Furniture, vol.1, 1987.

Scottish Cabinet Makers Price Book, 1805-1825. David Jones, in Reg. Furniture, vol.3, 1989.

Looking at Scottish Furniture, 1570-1900. David Jones, St. Andrews, 1987? ·

British Furniture Makers. John Gloag, 1945.

Domestic Life in Scotland, 1488-1688. John Warrack, London, 1920.

Kelly's Directory of Cabinet, Furniture and Upholstery Trades. [1877 - 1936].

Aberdeen

Oak Furniture. Victor Chinnery, Woodbridge 1986. [Aberdeen Furniture, 1580-1700.]

Edinburgh

A Dictionary of Edinburgh Furniture Makers. Francis Bamford, 1983.

Some Edinburgh Furniture Makers. Francis Bamford. B.O.T.O.E.C., vol.32, 1966.

OLD EDN CLUB.

The Edinburgh Branch of the Scottish National Union of Cabinet & Chair Makers, 1833-1837. Ian MacDougall. B.O.T.O.E.C., vol.33, 1969.

RECORDS ORIG N.L. W ED ROOM

The Edinburgh Furnishing Trade, 1708-1790. Sebastian Pryke, in Reg. Furniture, vol.3, 1989.

EDIN. SOC. OF CABINET & CHAIR MAKERS 1836—1874. 199 MEMBERS

CANDLEMAKERS

Edinburgh

The Incorporation of Candlemakers of Edinburgh, 1517-1884. W. Forbes Gray, B.O.T.O.E.C.vol.17, 1930.

CARRIERS

The 19th Century Scottish Carrier Trade. Arthur S. Morris, in Scott. Geog. Mag. vol.96, 1980.

CHARTERED ACCOUNTANTS

Scottish Chartered Accountants. Anna B.G. Dunlop, Scottish Genealogist, vol.12, 1965.

CHEMISTS

Kelly's Directory of Chemists & Druggists. [1869 - 1916].

The Registers of Pharmaceutical Chemists & Chemists & Druggists. [1880 - 1950].

The Chemists and Druggists Year Book and Directory for Scotland. [1914 - 1939].

The Chemical Directory & Pharmaceutists' Compendium. [1851].

The Registers of Pharmaceutical Chemists and Chemists and Druggists. [1880 - 1950].

CLOCK & WATCHMAKERS

General

Old Clockmakers in Scotland, 1453-1850. John Smith, Edinburgh, 1921.

Andrew Dickie & Others, clock & watchmakers. Martin Norgate, in Antiq. Horol., vol.11, 1979.

Scottish Clockmakers: [a brief history up to 1900] Felix Hudson, Dunfermline, 1984.

British Clocks & Clockmakers. Kenneth Ullyett, 1948.

The Early Clockmakers of Great Britain. Brian Loomes, London 1981.

Clocks of the British Isles. Felix Hudson. [pt. 2: North of the Border, in Clocks vol. 6 nos. 10 & 11, 1984.]

Grandfather Clocks & their Cases. [some Scottish clocks]. Brian Loomes, Newton Abbot, 1985.

Bitten's Old Clocks & Watches & their Makers. 9th ed. by Cecil Clutton. 16th ed. Richard Good.

Longcase-engraved dials: mid-Scotland. Felix Hudson, in Antiq. Horol. vol.12, 1980.

Kelly's Directory of the Watch & Clock Trades. Kelly & Co., London, 1872 - 1937. [16 directories].

The Watchmaker, jeweller, Silversmith & Optician Annual Directory of Trade Marks, Trade Names & Punch Marks. [1931 - 1967].

Arbroath

George Smith's Clocks. I.A.N. Henderson, in Scots. Mag., vol.108, 1977.

Dunfermline

Dunfermline Clockmakers up to 1900. Jean & Martin Norgate and Felix Hudson, Dunfermline, 1982.

Hamilton

Marking time in Hamilton: 300 years of Hamilton watches and clocks. William Wallace, Hamilton, 1981.

Stirling

Old Stirling Clockmakers, Charles Allan, 1990, Stirling.

CLOG-MAKERS

The Clogman of Balmaclellan. Sallyanne Duncan, Scots Mag. vol.125, 1986.

COALMINERS

A General View of the Coal Trade in Scotland. [including an inquiry into the condition of the women who carry coals underground.] Robert Bald, Edinburgh, 1812.

A History of the Scottish Coal Industry, vol.1, 1700-1815. Baron F. Duckham, Newton Abbot, 1970.

The Scottish Miners. R. Page Arnot, London, 1955.

Scottish Coalmining Ancestors. L.S.Reeks, Baltimore, 1986.

Mining in Mid & East Lothian, history from the earliest time to the present. Andrew S. Cunningham, Edinburgh, 1925.

COMMISSIONERS OF SUPPLY

The Commissioners of Supply for Dumfriesshire, 1692 - 1711. W.A.J. Prevost, Trans. of Dumfries & Galloway Nat. Hist. & Antiq. Soc. vol.36.

CONFECTIONERS

Kelly's Directory of the Grocery, Oil and Colour trades including confectionary, tobacco and provision trades of England, Scotland & Wales. [1872 - 1922].

Confectionary Trade Directory of trade marks & trade names. [1930 - 1941].

CONSTABLES

A sketch history of the High Constables of Edinburgh. J.D. Marwick, Edinburgh, 1865.

The Society of the High Constables of Edinburgh. Year Books. [List members & Moderators; from ? - date.]

COOPERS

The Incorporation of Coopers Glasgow. Glasgow, 1880.

CORDINERS

General

The Romance of the shoe; the history of shoemaking in all ages, especially in England and Scotland. Thomas Wright, 1922.

Ayrshire

The Ayrshire Boot & Shoe Industry, 1839-1939. Brenda M. White, in Scott. Indust. Hist., vol. 7.2, 1984.

Canongate

The Incorporation of Cordiners of the Canongate, 1538-1773. C.A.Malcolm, B.O.T.O.E.C.,vol.18, 1932.

Glasgow

History of the Incorporation of Cordiners in Glasgow. W. Campbell, Glasgow, 1883.

Perth

The shoemaker Incorporation of Perth, 1545 to 1927. Peter Baxter, Perth, 1927.

St. Andrews

The Cordinars of St. Andrews. D.H. Fleming, reprint from St. Andrews Citizen, 5th April, 1879.

Stirling

The Incorporation of shoemakers of Stirling. David B. Morris, Stirling, 1925.

COVENANTERS

The Scottish Covenanters, 1660-1688. Ian B. Cowan, London, 1976. [this work contains a useful bibliography].

The Covenanters of Ayrshire. R. Lawson, Paisley, 1887.

History of the Sufferings of the Church of Scotland. Robert Wodrow, 1721-1722.

Men of the Covenant. A. Smellie, 1911.

The Covenanters. J.K. Hewison, 1908.

The Scottish Covenanters. James Barr, 1947.

Napthali; or the wrestlings of the church of Scotland for the kingdon of Christ. 1693.

Biographia Presbyteriana. Patrick Walker, Edinburgh, 1827.

Six saints of the Covenant. Patrick Walker, 1901.

The Covenanters in Moray & Ross. M. Macdonald, Inverness, 1892.

The Covenanters of the Merse. J.W. Brown, Edinburgh, 1893.

CRIMINALS

A selected bibliography on highwaymen, outlaws, pirates and smugglers. Compiled by R. Cameron, Mitchell Library, 1983.

Notable Dundee Trials. A.H. Millar, in People's Journal, 1905.

Criminal Trials in Scotland, 1488 - 1624, 3 vols.. Robert Pitcairn, Bannantyne Club, Edinburgh, 1833.

DENTISTS

The Dental Directory. [1909 - 1915].

Dental Surgeons Directory. [1877 - 1925:- 58th annual issue].

DOCTORS, PHYSICIANS & SURGEONS

General

History of Scottish Medicine to 1860. John Dixon Comrie, 2nd. edition, 1930, 2 volumes.

Dynasties of Doctors. Douglas Guthrie, Scottish Genealogist, volume 5, no. 2, April 1958.

List of the Members of the Royal Colleges of Physicians of the U.K.. Royal College of Physicians of Edinburgh, Edinburgh, 1981.

Roll of commissioned officers in the medical service of the British Army, 1727 - 1898. Aberdeen University Press, 1917.

British Doctors in Russia, 1657-1807. J.H. Appleby, Norwich, 1979.

Doctors, Bodies & snatchers. Hector Bryson, Edinburgh, 1978.

Aberdeen

Early Deeside Doctors. George P. Milne, in Aberdeen Univ. Rev., vol.48, 1980.

Aberdeen doctors at home and abroad. E.H.B. Rodger, Edinburgh, 1893.

Angus

10 Tayside Doctors. J.S.G.Blair, Edinburgh, 1990.

Edinburgh

Pharmacy and Medicine in Old and New Edinburgh. C.G. Drummond, Scottish Genealogist, volume 12, no. 1, May 1965.

History of the Royal College of Physicians of Edinburgh. W.S. Craig, Oxfoed, Blackwell, 1976. [lists Hon. fellows & members 1696-1975; office bearers 1681-1975].

Historical Sketch & Laws of the Royal College of Physicians of Edinburgh from its institution to 1925. Edinburgh, 1925. [lists fellows 1681-1925 with name; date of their diploma; place where they received a degree; date of licence to practise; date of admission as fellow].

Card index of Edinburgh University MDs, compiled by J.D. Comrie. [Name; title of thesis; date of same] In library of the Royal College of Physicians of Edinburgh.

Medical Society of Edinburgh. General list of members. Edinburgh, 1850, supplement 1855.

Royal College of Surgeons of Edinburgh, list of fellows, 1581 - 31 December, 1873. Edinburgh, 1874.

Royal College of Physicians of Edinburgh list of Fellows, members & licentiates of the college. Edinburgh, 1868 - 1884 & 1886; supplements 1888, 1890.

Glasgow

Catalogue of the Library of the College of Physicians and Surgeons of Glasgow. 2 Volumes, 1885 - 1901. [Contains a list of medical practitioners in the Western district of Scotland.

Memorials of the faculty of Physicians and Surgeons of Glasgow, 1599 - 1850. Alexander Duncan, Glasgow, 1896.

Sketch of the History of the Faculty of Physicians and Surgeons, Glasgow. W. Weir, Glasgow, 1864; also 1868.

University of Glasgow, Faculty of Medicine Year books, 1949 - 1955; 1957. [These contain name, photograph and quote of each person.]

Historical Sketch of the Glasgow Southern Medical Society. John Dougall, Glasgow, 1988.

Kelso

The Doctors of Kelso. J.L. Trainer, Berwick, n.d.

East India Company

> A History of the Indian Medical Service, 1600 - 1913, 2 volumes. Dirom Grey Crawford, 1914.
>
> Roll of the Indian Medical Service, 1615 - 1930. Dirom Grey Crawford, 1930.
>
> Medical Officers of the Indian Army, 1764 - 1838. Edward Dodwell and James Samuel Miles, 1839.

DYERS & BONNET-MAKERS

> The Incorporation of Dyers and Bonnet-makers in Glasgow. W.H. Hill, Glasgow, 1875.
>
> The young dyers of Galashiels. P. Sulley, Galashiels, 1919.

ECCLESIASTICS

General

> Papers of British Churchmen, 1780 - 1940. H.M.S.O., 1987.
>
> An interim list of the heads of some Scottish Monastic houses before c. 1300. A.A.M. Duncan, in Bibliotheck, ii, 4-27.
>
> The priory of St Mary's Isle. [Contains lists of priors etc.] R.C. Reid, Trans. of Dumfries & Galloway Nat. Hist. & Antiq. Soc.

Presbyterians

> The Reformed Presbyterian Church in Scotland, its Congregations, Ministers and Students, William James Couper, Edinburgh 1925.
>
> Sketch of the History of the First Reformed Presbyterian Congregation. Thomas Binnie, Paisley, 1888.
>
> History of the Congregations of the United Presbyterian Church from 1733 - 1900. Robert Small, Edinburgh 1904.

Baptists

> A Short History of Baptists in Scotland. W.J.Seaton, Dunstable, c.1983.
>
> History of the Baptists in Scotland. George Yuille, Glasgow, 1926.

Congregationalists

> A History of Congregational Independency in Scotland. James Ross, Glasgow, 1900.

Episcopalians

History of the Episcopal Church in the Diocese of Moray.
J.B. Craven, London, 1889.

The Episcopal History of Perth, 1689-1894. George T.S.
Farquhar, Perth, 1894.

Catholics

Catholic Directory for Scotland, 1829 - 1975. D. McRoberts,
Glasgow, 1976.

The Catholic Hierarchy of Scotland: a biographical list.
James Darragh, Glasgow, 1986.

Ministers

Fasti Ecclesiae Scoticanae, by Hew Scott, revised by
W.S.Crockett and Sir Francis J. Grant, volume 9 edited
by J.A.Lamb. 10th vol. ed. Donald Farquhar Macleod
Macdonald, Edinburgh, 1981.

Fasti Ecclesiae Scoticanae Medii Aevi to 1638. D.E.R. Watt,
Scottish Record Society, Edinburgh, 1969.

Scottish parish clergy at the Reformation, 1540-1574.
Charles H. Haws, Scottish Record Society, Edinburgh,
1972.

Fasti of the United Free Church of Scotland, 1900-1929. John
A. Lamb, Edinburgh, 1956.

Ministers to the soldiers of Scotland. vol.2, 1856-1945.
A.C. Dow, Edinburgh, 1983? Limited ed. of 4 copies.

Register of Ministers & Readers in the Kirk of Scotland,
1574. Woodrow Society Miscellany 1, 1844.

Register of Minister, exhorters & readers and of their
stipends, 1567. Alexander Macdonald, Maitland Club,
Edinburgh, 1830.

Fathers of Independence, or Biographical Sketches of Early
Scottish Congregational Ministers, 1798 - 1851. Robert
Kinniburgh, Edinburgh 1851.

Some noted ministers of the Northern Highlands. D. Wick
Beaton, Inverness, 1929.

Biographies of Highland Clergymen. Inverness, 1889.

Clergy lists of the Highland district. F. Forbes & W.J.
Anderson in Innes Review, vol.17, 129-184.

The ministers of Glasgow & their churches. John J. Rae, nd.

List of emigrant ministers to America, 1690 - 1811. Gerald
Fothergill, 1904.

Abbots

The Abbots of Deir. Scottish Notes & Queries, iii. 55. 1889.

The Abbots of the Scottish Monastery at Würzburg. Scottish Notes and Queries, ii. 20-21, 1888.

Bishops

The Bishops of Scotland, John Dowden, Glasgow, 1912.

Catalogue of Bishops of several Sees of Scotland to 1688, with account of religious houses in Scotland at the time of the Reformation. R. Keith, 1755.

The Archbishops of St. Andrews. J. Herkless & R.K. Hannay, 5 vols., Edinburgh, 1907-1915.

The Appointment of Bishops in Scotland during the medieval period. J. Dowden, Scottish Historical Review, vol.7, 1910.

Bishops of Aberdeen. H. Boece, 1522. New Spalding Club, 1894.

The Bishops of Dunkeld. J. Dowden, 2vols., Scottish Historical Review, vol.1, 1904, vol.2, 1905.

Bishop of the Scottish Episcopal Church in Fife: an historical catalogue of the Scottish Bishops, Robert Keith, Edinburgh, 1824.

The Bishops of Glasgow. J. Dowden, Scottish Historical Review, vol.5, 1908.

A Catalogue of the Bishops of Orkney, Professor. Münch of Christiania. Bannantyne Club miscellany, iii, Edinburgh, 1855.

History of the church in Orkney, 1558 - 1688, 2 vols., including the bishops of Orkney. J.B. Craven, 1897.

From Samson to Gregory: the Bishops and Clergy of Brechin, c.1150-1250. David G. Adams, in Book Soc. Friends Brechin Cathedral, no.34, 1985.

The Medieval Bishops of Dunblane and their Church. James Hutchison Cockburn, Edinburgh, 1959.

Rentale Dunkeldense: Being an account of the Bishopric, 1505-1517, with Myln's lives of the bishops, 1483-1517. Robert Kerr Hannay, Edinburgh, Scottish History Society, 1915.

Saints

Calendar of Scottish saints from Aberdeen Matyrology. D. Laing, Edinburgh, 1859.

Kalendars of Scottish Saints. Alexander Penrose Forbes, Edinburgh, 1872.

A Calendar of Scottish Saints. Dom Michael Barrett, Fort
    Augustus, 1904.

The saints of Scotland. Edwin S. Towill, Edinburgh, 1983.

Aberdeen

The Aberdeen pulpit and universities. Sketches of Aberdeen
    clergy and professors in the College. J. Bruce,
    Aberdeen, 1844.

The Aberdeen doctors, a notable group of Scottish
    theologians of the first episcoplan period, 1610-1683.
    D. Macmillan, London, 1909.

Eminent Divines in Aberdeen and the North: their work and
    influence. J. Martin, Aberdeen, 1888.

Old Aberdeenshire Ministers and their people. John Davidson,
    Aberdeen, 1895.

Ayr

Ayrshire parish clerks. D.A. McKay, in Ayrshire coll. vol.7,
    39 - 46.

Caithness

Memorials of Caithness Ministers. A. Auld, Edinburgh, 1912.

Edinburgh

The Kirks of Edinburgh, 1560-1984. A. Ian Dunlop, Scottish
    Record Society, Edinburgh, 1989.

Glasgow

A Historical Sketch of the United Free Church, Glasgow: with
    a complete alumnus roll from 1856 - 1929. W.M.Macgregor
    & B. Blake, Glasgow, 1930.

St. Andrews

Register of the ministers, Elders, and Deacons of the
    Christian Congregation of St. Andrews. D.H. Fleming,
    Ecott. Hist. Soc., 2 vols., Edinburgh 1889-1890.

Skye

The Clerical Sons of Skye. Donald Portree MacKinnon,
    Dingwall, 1930.

Papers of British Churchmen, 1780 - 1940. H.M.S.O., 1987.

ELECTORS

[Most burghs should have lists of those eligible to vote
from 1832 onwards. If they are not listed below, it is worth
checking with the local libraries.]

List of Freeholders & Electors [of Aberdeen]. Aberdeen, 1832.

Dunfermline Burgh voters rolls. [1832 - 1970].

List of Freeholders & Electors [of Edinburgh]. Edinburgh, 1832.

Western Fife voters roll. [1846 & 1860].

List of Freeholders & Electors [of Glasgow]. Glasgow, 1832.

List of Freeholders & Electors of Midlothian. 1832

ELECTRICIANS

The Electricians' Directory. [1883 - 1885].

The Electrical Trades' Directory & Handbook. [1883 - 1950].

Directory of the Electrical Industry. [1893].

The Electrician. Electrical Trades Directory & Handbook. [1894 - 1967].

The Electrical Engineers' Central-station Directory. [1896 - 1907].

Kelly's Directory of the Electrical Industry, Wireless and allied trades. [1924 - 1926].

EMIGRANTS

Dictionary of Scottish Emigrants to the U.S.A., 2 vols. Donald Whyte, Baltimore, 1972 & supplement, 1986.

Dictionary of Scottish Emigrants to Canada before confederation. Donald Whyte, Toronto, 1986.

Directory of Scottish Settlers in North America, 1625 - 1825. 6 vols. David Dobson, Baltimore.

Scots in the Carolinas. David Dobson, Baltimore, 1986.

Scottish American Heirs, David Dobson, Baltimore, 1990.

The Original Scots Colonists, 1612 - 1783. David Dobson, Baltimore, 1989.

American Vital Records from the Gentleman's Magazine, 1731 - 1868. David Dobson, Baltimore, 1987.

List of emigrant ministers to America, 1690 - 1811. Gerald Fothergill, 1904.

Undertakers in Scotland of the Ulster Plantation, 1609. David Masson, 1887, in introduction to the Register of the Privy Council, 1st ser., viii.

The Caledonian Phalanx: Scots in Russia. Paul Dukes, Edinburgh 1987.

Scots in "little London". [Gothenburg]. Goran Behre, in Northern Scotland, vol.7, no.2, 1987.

Scots in Russia in the 17th & 18th Centuries. Kenneth Macleod, in J. Russ. Stud., no.46, 1983.

Burgesses & settlers in Danzig, Posen etc., 1531 – 1768. The Scots in west & east Prussia. Th. A. Fischer, 1903.

Scots admitted to the citizenship of Cracow, with evidence regarding their parentage, 1579 – 1702. Scottish History Society, no.59, 1915.

The Scots Overseas: a selected bibliography. Donald Whyte, Federation of Family History Societies, 1988.

ENGINEERS

General

Famous Names in Engineering. James Carvill, London, 1981.

Lives of the Engineers. 5 vols. S. Smiles, 1874. New ed. 1891.

Blower's Architects', Surveyors', Engineers' & Builders' Directory. [1860].

The Architects', Engineers' and Building Trades' Directory. [1868].

Kelly's Directory of the Engineers & Iron & Metal Trades. [1870 – 1940].

The Engineer Directory. [1895 – 1950].

The Directory of Shipowners, ship builders and marine engineers. [1903 – 1950].

Engineers' address register. [1907 – 1917].

The All-British Engineering and building trades directory. [1915].

Engineering Directory. [1918 – 1938].

Paisley

A survey of early Paisley engineers. Sylvia Clark, in Scott. Ind. Hist., vol.6, 1984.

ENTERTAINERS

The good auld days: the story of Scotland's entertainers from music hall to television. Gordon Irving, London, 1977.

The Dramatic & Musical Directory of the United Kingdom.
[1883 - 1893].

EXCISEMEN

Burns' Excise Associates. John Fowler Mitchell, Scottish
Genealogist, vol. 6, nos. 1 & 2, 1959; vol.7, no.2,
1960.

EXPLORERS

Africa Explored: Europeans in the Dark Continent, 1769-1889.
Christopher Hibbert, London, 1982.

FACTORS

The Wilsons. A Banffshire family of Factors. Andrew C.
Brown, Edinburgh, 1936.

FANCIERS

The Fanciers Directory containing the names & addresses of
all judges & Exhibitions of Dogs, Poultry, Pigeons,
Cage birds, Rabbits & Cats in the U.K. [1879].

FISH-WORKERS & FISHERMEN

Sea Changes: the fisher quines of Peterhead. Alison Buchan,
in Leopard, no.122, 1987.

St. Andrews fishermen and the pressgang in 1759 & 1760. D.H.
Fleming, St. Andrews, 1904.

Society of Free Fishermen of Newhaven. James Wilson,
Newhaven, 1951.

The British Fisheries Society, 1786-1893. Jean Dunlop,
Edinburgh, 1978.

FLESHERS

Glasgow

The Incorporation of Fleshers of Glasgow. Glasgow, 1869.

Stirling

The Incorporation of Fleshers of Stirling. David B. Morris,
Stirling, 1921.

FREEMASONS

The Complete Manual of Freemasonry. William Harvey, 17th
ed., Glasgow, 1980.

Royal Order of Scotland. Keith B. Jackson, in his 'Beyond the Craft', London, 1980.

Our Predecessors: Scottish Masons of about 1600. A.C.F. Jackson, in Ars Quatuor Coronatorum, vol.91, 1978.

Edinburgh

A unique craft: Edinburgh masons in the 17th century. David Stevenson, in Scotia, vol.11, 1987.

Kirkwall

Lodge Kirkwall Kilwinning: the story from 1736. James Flett, Lerwick, 1976.

FURRIERS

Scottish Fur Traders in Canada, 1750-1850. Mary Black-Rogers. in Ethnohist, vol.33, no.4, 1986.

The Development of the Voyageur Contract, 1686-1821. Lawrence M. Lande, Montreal, 1989.

Glasgow

History of the Skinners, Furriers and Glovers of Glasgow. Harry Lumsden, Glasgow, 1937.

GARDENERS

East Lothian

Ancient Fraternity of Free Gardners of East Lothian. Charles Martine, ed. W.H. Brown, in E.Lothian Antiquarian & Field Naturalist Society Trans.

Glasgow

The History of the Incorporation of Gardeners of Glasgow, 18.11.1626 - 1.9.1903. Introduction P. Baird McNab, clerk, Glasgow, 1903.

GEOLOGISTS

History of the Geological Society of Glasgow, 1858-1908. Peter MacNair & Frederick Mort, Glasgow, 1908.

GLASS MAKERS & ENGRAVERS

The Jacobite Engravers. G.B.Seddon, in The Glass Circle, edited by R.J.Charleston, Wendy Evans, Ada Polak, London, 1979.

Scottish & Jacobite Glass. Arnold Fleming, Glasgow, 1938, rep. Wakefield, 1977.

Scotland's Glass Industry. Colin M. Brown, in Scott. Geogr. Mag. vol.96, 1980.

Glass: art nouveau to art deco. [includes Scottish makers]. Victor Arwas, London, 1977.

Pottery Gazette & Glass Trade Review Directory. [1905 - 1950].

Directory for the British Glass Industry. [1923 - 1965].

Brian J M Hardyman, 26 St. Anne's Drive, Coalpit Heath, Bristol, BS17 2TH, is compiling an index of British glassmakers. He has a card index running to many thousands of names. He would be happy to receive information about glassmakers and will answer questions if you write to him enclosing a stamped, addressed envelops.

GOLFERS

The Aberdeen Golfers. C. Smith, London, 1910.

GLOVERS

Kelso

The Kelso Glovers' Book. James F. Leishman, History of the Berwickshire Naturalists' Club, vol.25, Edinburgh, 1927.

Glasgow

History of the Skinners, Furriers and Glovers of Glasgow. Harry Lumsden, Glasgow, 1937.

Perth

The Annals of the Glover Incorporation of Perth, 1300-1905. George J.P. Wilson, Perth, 1905; 2nd ed. 1985.

GOLDSMITHS and SILVERSMITHS

General

Jackson's Silver & Gold Marks. Ed. Ian Pickford, 1989. First pub. 1905.

Women Silversmiths, 1685 - 1845, Philippa Glanville & Jennifer Faulds Goldsborough, Thames & Hudson, London, 1990.

Scottish Provincial Silver. Frederick Graham, in Landowning in Scot., no.194, 1983.

Directory of British Manufacturers of Jewellery, Silver, electroplate. [1918].

Banff

Goldsmiths & Silversmiths of the Royal Burgh of Banff, 1600 - 1850, J.R.Salter, 1980, [Scottish Provincial Silversmiths - occasional papers.]

Dumfries

Dumfries Silversmiths, - Kirkpatrick H. Dobie, Dumfries, c.1984

Edinburgh

The Incorporation of Goldsmiths of the City of Edinburgh. Stuart Maxwell. University of Edinburgh journal, 33 no.1, 1987.

The Lovable Craft, 1687-1987. Catalogue of an exhibition. George Dalgleish & Stuart Maxwell, Edinburgh 1987.

Forres

Goldsmiths & Silversmiths of Forres, 1600 - 1860, J.R.Salter, 1980. [Scott. Prov. Silversmiths].

Fortrose

Goldsmiths & Silversmiths in Fortrose, 1730 - 1790, J.R.Salter, 1980. [Scott. Prov. Silversmiths].

Inverness

Inverness Silversmiths, M.O.McDougall, Inverness, 1979.

Paisley

Incorporation of Hammermen in Paisley and its Silversmiths, J.R.Salter, 1980, [Scott. Prov. Silversmiths].

Perth

A History of Perth Silver, J. Mundy, Perth, 1980.

Tain

Tain Silversmiths, 1650 - 1850, J.R.Salter, 1980. [Scott. Prov. Silversmiths.]

GROCERS

The grocer Company of Glasgow, 1789-1934. John H. Stevenson, Glasgow, n.d.

Kelly's Directory of the Grocery, Oil and Colour Trades including Confectionary, Tobacco & Provision Trades of England, Scotland and Wales. [1872 - 1922].

Grocery & the Provision Merchant Directory of Brands, Trademarks and Trade Names. [1930 - 1941].

HAMMERMEN

General

Old Pewter, its Makers & Marks, Howard H. Cotterell, London, 1929. Reprinted 1963.

Scottish Pewterware & Pewterers, L. Ingleby Wood, 1907.

Canongate

The Hammermen of the Canongate. Marguerite Wood, B.O.T.O.E.C., vols. 19 & 20, 1933 & 1935.

Dunfermline

Miscellaneous records of the Dunfermline Hammermen, (17th & 18th century), collated by Daniel Thomson, 1901. [ms., Dunfermline Library].

The Dunfermline Hammermen. Daniel Thomas, Paisley, 1909.

Records of the Dunfermline Hammermen, 1585 - 1686. N.L. Anderson, 1961.

Edinburgh

The Edinburgh Touchplates, Lt. Col. J.S. Bisset, Antique Collector, September 1939.

A historical account of the Hammermen of Edinburgh. W.C. Little, Arch. Scot. vol.1, Edinburgh, 1792.

The Hammermen of Edinburgh and their altar in St. Giles' Church, 1494-1558. J. Smith, Edinburgh, 1905.

Glasgow

Traditions & Customs of the Hammermen of Glasgow, and the insignia and relics of the Incorporation of Hammermen. Arthur Muir, Glasgow, 1923.

History of the Hammermen of Glasgow. H. Lumsden & P.H. Aitken, Paisley, 1912, 2nd. ed. 1915.

Paisley

Incorporation of Hammermen in Paisley and its Silversmiths, J.R.Salter, 1980, [Scott. Prov. Silversmiths].

Haddington

Incorporation of Hammermen of Haddington. James H. Jamieson, in East Lothian Antiquarian & Field Naturalists Scoiety Trans., 1934.

Perth

The Perth Hammermen Book, 1518 - 1568. C.A. Hunt, Perth, 1889.

The Incorporation of Hammermen of Stirling, David B. Morris, Stirling, 1927.

Old Minute Book of Stirling Incorporation of Hammermen. W.B. Cook, Trans. Stirl. Nat. Hist. & Arch. Soc. 1901-2.

HEIRS

Records of Retours, 1530 - 1700, 3 vols., London ?, 1811 - 1816.

Services of Heirs, 1700 - to date. Published in Edinburgh.

Scottish American Heirs, David Dobson, Baltimore, 1990.

HOSIERS

The Borders Hosiery & knitwear industry:1770-1970. Clifford Gulvin, Selkirk, 1979.

The Scottish Hosiery & knitwear industry, 1680-1980. Clifford Gulvin, Edinburgh, 1984.

Skinners' Hosiery & Knit Goods Directory. [1947 - 1950].

HOSPITALERS

The Hospitalers in Scotland in the 15th century. John Edward, Scottish Historical Review, vol.9, 1912.

INSURERS & INSURANCE BROKERS

The Edinburgh Recorder. J. Gilhooley, 1990. [A list of about 5000 Edinburgh policy holders, 1720 - 1840].

The British Fire Mark, 1680-1879. Brian Wright, Cambridge, 1982.

The Sun Alliance Insurance Office, 1710-1960. P.G.M. Dickson, Oxf. Univ. Press, 1960.

The Directory of Insurance Brokers. [1922 - 1950].

IRON & STEEL TRADES

Ryland's Iron, Steel and Allied Trades Directory with brands & trademarks. [1881 - 1950].

Iron & Steel Directory & Handbook. [1930 - 1950].

JURORS

List of Jurors 1604-1900. David Littlejohn, New Spalding Club, Miscellany 2, 1908.

KEELMEN

Newcastle Keelmen in the 18th Century: The Scottish Connection. Harry D. Watson, Scottish Genealogist, vol.34, no.4, 1987.

LAUNDERERS

The Laundry Trade Directory and launderers handbook. [1908].

Kelly's Directory of the laundery and allied trades. [1934, 1938].

LAWYERS & LAWMEN

General

The Faculty of Advocates in Scotland, 1532 - 1943: with genealogical notes. Sir Frances James Grant, Edinburgh 1944. Scottish Record Office Publication, part 15.

The Faculty of Advocates, Biographical dictionary of Members admitted, 1800-1986. Stephen P. Walker. Edinburgh, n.d.

The Minute Book of the Faculty of Advocates, 1661-1750. 2 vols. Ed. John MacPherson Pinkerton, Stair Society, 1976 & 1980.

The Lord Advocates of Scotland, 1483 - 1880. George William Thomson Omond, 3 volumes, 1883 - 1914.

The Lord Chancellors of Scotland, 2 vols.. S. Cowan, 1911.

History of the Writers to H.M. Signet ... with list of Members from 1594 - 1935. nd. edition, Edinburgh 1936.

The Society of Writer to H.M. Signet. Hector McKechnie, 1936.

Senators of the College of Justice, 1532 - 1850. G.Brunton & D.Haig, Edinburgh, n.d..

Senators of the College of Justice, 1569-1578. P.G.B. McNeil, in Juridicial Review, new series 5, 120-124.

Office of Master of Requests. P.G.B. McNeil. [includes a list of holders of the office, 1514-1649]. Juridicial Review, new series, 4, 210-213.

List of Scottish Sheriffs to circa 1300. Professor D.W.Hunter Marshall, 1959. [Typescript in Scottish Record Office].

Sheriffs of Scotland to circa 1306. G.W.S.Barrow, n.d. [Typescript at S.R.O.].

The Hereditary Sheriffs of Galloway. 2 vols. Sir A. Agnew, Edinburgh, 1893.

The S.S.C. Story, 1784-1984. R.B.Barclay, Edinburgh, 1984.

The Clerk of the Privy Council. [includes a list of holders, 1549-1708]. P.G.B. McNeil, in Juridicial Review, new series, 7, 135-150.

Aberdeenshire

Notices of the Officials of the Sheriff Court of Aberdeenshire: New Spalding Club, vols. 28,31,32, Aberdeen 1904 - 1907.

History of the Society of Advocates in Aberdeen. John Alexander Henderson, New Spalding Club, volume 40, 1912.

Dumfriesshire

The Commissioners of supply for Dumfriesshire, 1692-1711. W.A.J. Prevost in Dumfries & Galloway Nat. Hist. & Antiq. Soc. vol. 36, 27-51.

Kirkcudbright

Commissioners of supply for the Stewartry of Kirkcudbright, 1728-1828. C.A.S. Maitland, Castle Douglas, 1934.

Lanarkshire

The minutes of the Justices of Peace for Lanarkshire, 1707-1723. Charles A. Malcolm, Scottish History Society, Edinburgh, 1931.

LEAD MINING

The Ancient Lead Mining Industry of Islay. R.M.Callendar, Islay Museums Trust, 1981?

The Ancient metal mines of the isle of Islay, Argyll. R.M.Callendar & J. Macaulay, in Br. Min. no.24, 1984.

Miners' Bargains [lead mines]. W.S. Harvey & G. Downs-Rose, in British Mining, no.34, 1987.

LIGHTHOUSES

Clyde Lighthouses, 1756 - 1956. George Blake, Glasgow, 1956.

MASONS

The Master Masons to the Crown of Scotland. Rev. R.S.Mylne, Edinburgh 1893.

Scottish Stone masons in Texas. Donald Whyte, Scottish Genealogist, vol.13, 1966.

Scottish Stone cutters & Blacksmiths who came to Texas, 1880. Robert W. Baumgardner, Aberdeen & N.E. Scotland F.H.S. Journal, no.22, 1987.

Dundee

The 3 United Trades of Dundee: masons, wrights, slaters. Annette M. Smith. Abertay Historical Society, 1987.

Glasgow

Sketch of the Incorporation of Masons, and the Lodge of Glasgow. J. Cruickshank, Glasgow, 1879.

Incorporation of Masons of Glasgow. W. Anderson Eadie, Glasgow, 1927.

MERCHANTS

Scottish Merchants and Traders in 17th & 18th century Warsaw. Anna Bieganska, in Scott. Slav. Rev., no.5, 1985.

The Scottish Merchant Community, 1690-1730. T.M. Devine, London, 1980.

Trade & Traders: some links between the ports of Montrose & Arbroath, 1742-1830. J.G.Duncan, in North, Scot., vol.7, 1986.

Scottish Traders in Virginia, 1750 - 1775. J.H. Soltow, in Econ. Hist. Review, 2nd series, no.12, 83-98.

Aberdeen

The economic activities of the Aberdeen Merchant Guild, 1750-1799. Tom Donnelly, in Scot. Econ. Soc. Hist., vol.1, 1981.

Beith

Beith - its merchants and others. Godfrey W. Iredell, Scottish Genealogist, vol.35, 1988.

Dundee

Dundee Register of Merchants and trades. Dundee, 1782. facsimile reprint, 1879.

Edinburgh

The Company of Merchants of the City of Edinburgh, 1681-1981. Nancy H. Miller, Edinburgh, 1981.

Members of the Edinburgh Merchants Company, 1687. The Scottish Antiquary, xii, 1898.

The Company of Merchants of the city of Edinburgh. H.M. Harvey-Jamieson, Scottish Genealogist, vol.8, 1961.

The rise and progress of the Company of Merchants of the City of Edinburgh, 1681-1902. A.Heron, Edinburgh, 1903.

Historical notes regarding the Merchant Company of Edinburgh, and the Widow's Scheme and Hospitals. A.K.Mackie, Edinburgh, 1862.

Glasgow

The Merchants' House of Glasgow. [a list of those matriculated]. W.H. Hill, Glasgow, 1868; also 1874.

Records of the Trades Houses of Glasgow, 1605 - 1678. ed. H. Lumsden, Glasgow, 1910.

View of the Merchants' House of Glasgow. A. Orr Ewing, Glasgow, 1866.

View of the history, constitution, and funds of the Guildry and Merchants' House Glasgow. James Ewing, Glasgow, 1817.

Stirling

The Stirling Merchant Gild and the life of John Cowan. David B. Morris, Stirling, 1919.

MILITARY

General

The Scots Army 1661 - 1688. Charles Dalton, Edinburgh, 1909.

A Military history of Perthshire, 1660 - 1902. Marchioness Tullibardine, Perth, 1908.

Names of Officers serving in the Scots Army in Scotland, with notes and memoirs. Charles Dalton, "Scots Army", 1909.

Soldiering & sailoring in the north-east of Scotland. J.M. Bulloch, Aberdeen University Library Bulletin, no.14, 1916.

Dundee court martial records, 1651. Godfrey Davies. Scottish History Society miscellany, vol.3, 1919.

History of the Royal Dragoons, 1661 - 1934. C.T. Atkinson, Glasgow, 1934.

History of the 17th (Northern) Division. A. Hilliard Atteridge, Glasgow, 1930.

The Lowland Scots Regiments, Their Origin, Character & Services previous to the Great War of 1914. Herbert Maxwell, Glasgow, 1918.

History of the Scottish Regiments. William Pratt Paul, Glasgow, n.d..

The Scots Men-at-arms & Life Guards in France from their formation until their final dissolution, 1418 - 1830. Wm. Forbes Leith, 1882.

The Story of the Highland Regiments, 1725 - 1925. Frederick Watson, London, 1925.

The Scottish regiments of the British Army. I.M. Mackay-Scobie, Edinburgh, 1942.

The story of the Border Regiment, 1939 - 1945. Philip J. Shears, London, 1948.

Old Scottish Regimental Colours. Andrew Ross, Edinburgh, 1885.

Papers illustrating the history of the Scots Brigade in the service of the United Netherlands, 1572 - 1782, 3 vols. James Ferguson, Edinburgh, 1899.

The pipes of war; a record of the achievemnets of pipers of Scottish and overseas regiments during the war, 1914 - 1918. Sir Bruce Seton & John Grant, Glasgow, 1920 & 1928.

The history oy the 16th battalion (the Canadian Scottish) Canadian Expeditionary Force in the Great War, 1914 - 1919. H.M. Urquhart, New York, 1932.

A History of the 48th Highlanders of Canada, 1929 - 1956. K. Beattie, 1956.

Scottish Mercenaries in Europe, 1570-1640. I.Ross Bartlett, in Scott. Tradit., vol.13, 1984-1985.

Military Officer, Students, etc. The Scots in Sweden, Th. A. Fischer, 1907.

Communion Roll of the Old Scots Regiment in Holland. Scottish History Society, no. 38, 1901.

Scottish Highlanders and the American Revolution. G. Murray Logan, Halifax, N.S., 1976.

71st Highlanders in Massachusetts, 1776 - 1780. C. Campbell, in New England Hist. & Gen. Reg. vol. 113, 1-14 & 84-94.

Ministers to the Soldiers of Scotland, vol.2, 1856-1945. A.C.Dow, Edinburgh, 1962. Limited ed. of 4 copies.

Old Soldiers of the 18th Century. E.A. Gray, Scottish Genealogist, vol.36, 1989.

The Whippets: The Book of the 2nd Lowland Field Ambulance. Glasgow, 1919.

An Almanack of Scottish Regiments, 1912. ed. Mrs. Douglas Campbell.

A list of Colonels, Lieutenant Colonels, Majors, Captains, Lieutenants & ensigns of H.M. Forces on the British Establishment. London, 1740.

Succession of Colonels to all H.M. Land Forces from their rise to 1742. London, 1742 & 1744.

A List of the General & Field Officers as they rank in the army. London, 1754, 1756 - 1858.

The Army List. 1661 - 1991. [quarterly, monthly during the two World Wars.]

New Annual Army List. H.G. Hart, 1840 - 1915.

The Scottish Military Directory. Edinburgh, 1890.

War Office List, 1905 - 1964.

Air Force

Air Force List, 1918 - 1989.

Regiments

ARGYLL & SUTHERLAND HIGHLANDERS

History of the Argyll & Sutherland Highlanders. 1st Battalion, 1939 - 1945. F.C.C. Graham, 1948.

History of the 1st Battalion Princess Louise's Argyll & Sutherland Highlanders. H.G. Robley & P.J. Aubin, Cape Town, 1883.

History of the 91st Princess Louise's Argyllshire Highlanders. The 1st Battalion, 1794 - 1894. P. Groves, Edinburgh, 1894.

History of the 91st Argyllshire Highlanders, now the 1st Battalion Princess Louise's). R.P. Dunn-Pattison, 1910.

Banzai Attack Korea 1951. [A & S Highlanders 1st battalion]. Alistair Sinclair McLeod, Bognor Regis, 1981.

History of the Argyll & Sutherland Highlanders, 2nd Battalion (Thin Red Line): Malaya campaign, 1941 - 1942. I. MacA. Stewart, 1947.

History of the Argyll & Sutherland Highlanders, 2nd battalion, 1944 - 1945. W.L. McElwee, 1949.

Records of the Stirlingshire, Dumbarton, Clackmannan and Kinross Militia. Highland Borderers Light Infantry, now 3rd Battalion of the Argyll & Sutherland Highlanders. A.H. Middleton, Stirling, 1904.

History of the Argyll & Sutherland Highlanders 5th Battalion. 91st Anti-tank regiment, 1939 - 1945. D. Flower, 1950.

History of the Argyll & Sutherland Highlanders 6th
     Battalion, 93rd anti-tank regiment, R.A.. William P.
     Paul, London, 1949.

History of the Argyll & Sutherland Highlanders, 7th
     Battalion, from El Alamein to Germany. I.C. Cameron,
     1946.

History of the Argyll & Sutherland Highlanders, 8th
     Battalion, 1939 - 1947. A.D. Malcolm, 1949.

History of the Argyll & Sutherland Highlanders, 9th
     Battalion, 54th light anti aircraft regiment, 1939 -
     1945. F.R.P. Barker, Edinburgh, 1951.

Argyll & Sutherland Highlanders 9th battalion.
     Dumbartonshire men at the front.   James Forrester &
     Watson Crawford, Glasgow, 1978.

Dumbartonshire's Volunteers and the 9th battalion, Argyll &
     Sutherland Highlanders. Michael Taylor, Dumbarton,
     1982.

10th Battalion Argyll & Sutherland Highlanders, 1914 - 1919.
     Herbert G. Sotheby, London, 1931.

Soldiers died in the Great War, 1914 - 1919, part 70,
     Princess Louise's Argyll & Sutherland Highlanders.
     H.M.S.O., 1921.

Historical records of the 93rd The Sutherland Highlanders,
     1800 - 1890. James McVeigh, Dumfries, 1890.

THE BLACK WATCH (42nd)

Chronology & book of days of the 42nd Royal Highlanders, the
     Black Watch, 1729 - 1874. n.p., Edinburgh, 1880.

Officers of the Black Watch, 1725 - 1937. Neil McMicking,
     Perth, 1937.

History of the 42nd Royal Highlanders - The Black Watch,
     1729 - 1893. Percy Groves, Edinburgh, 1893.

The Black Watch; the Royal Highlanders. London, 1916.

A Brief History of the Royal Highland Regiment, the Black
     Watch. John Stewart, Edinburgh, 1924.

The Black Watch. L.M. Watt, n.d.

A concise account of the Black Watch and its movements.
     J.L.R. Samson, Salisbury, 1984.

The Black Watch at Tinconderoga. Frederick B. Richards, New
     York, 1916.

The Black Watch. Bernard Fergusson, London, 1950.

The Black Watch. The History of the Royal Highland Regiment.
E. & A. Linklater, London, 1977.

'Geordie & Jock', a short account of the Tyneside Scottish.
[Black Watch, 1st battalion Tyneside Scottish]. J.L.R.
Samson, Surrey, 1978.

The Kirk Session of the 1st battalion of the Black Watch,
1954 - 1979. Norman W. Drummond, Perth, 1979?

A History of the 6th Battalion The Black Watch, 1939 - 1945.
B.J.G. Madden, Perth, 1948.

A History of the Black Watch, 1914 - 1918. A.G. Wauchope,
1925.

The Black Watch, formerly 42nd & 73rd Foot: medal roll, 1801
- 1911. 1913.

BORDERERS

The K.O.S.B. in the Great War. Stair Gillon, Berwick upon
Tweed, 1930.

The War Story of the King's Own Scottish Borderers, 1939 -
1945. Hugh Gunning, 1948.

The History of the 3rd battalion King's Own Scottish
Borderers, 1798 - 1907. R.W. Weir, Dumfries, 1907.

King's Own Scottish Borderers, 4th battalion, war history,
1939 - 1945.

War Record of 4th King's Own Scottish Borderers and Lothians
and Border Horse. W. Sorley Brown, Galashiels, 1920.

War History of the 5th battalion King's Own Scottish
Borderers. G.F. Scott Elliot, 1928.

King's Own Scottish Borderers; a border battalion. The
History of the 7 - 8th (service) battalion K.O.S.B.,
1920.

Soldiers died in the Great War, 1914 - 1919, part 30, King's
Own Scottish Borderers. H.M.S.O., 1921.

CAMERON HIGHLANDERS (79th)

The Compassionate War [Queen's own Cameron Highlanders].
Hugh Davies, Abbottsbury Publications, 1980.

The raising of the 79th Highlanders. Loraine Maclean of
Dochgarroch, in Soc. of W. Highland & Island Historical
Research, 1980.

Souvenir booklet of the 6th Cameron Highlanders. London,
1916.

Cameron Highlanders: Officers present at the various campaigns, battles etc. Seymour Clarke, 1913.

Historical records of the 79th regiment of foot, or Cameron Highlanders. Robert Jamieson, Edinburgh, 1863.

Historical Records of the Queen's own Cameron Highlanders, 2 vols.. Edinburgh, 1909.

Charlie Company in service with C company 2nd Queen's Own Cameron Highlanders, 1940 - 1944. Peter Cochrane, London, 1977.

The 5th Camerons. J.H.F. Macewen, Edinburgh, 1938.

The History of the 7th battalion Queen's Own Cameron Highlanders. J.W. Sandilands, Stirling, 1922.

War Office. Soldiers died in the Great War, 1914 - 1919. Part 66, H.M.S.O., 1931

CAMERONIANS

Regimental Standing Orders of the Cameronians. Hamilton, 1930.

The History of the Cameronians (Scottish Rifles), vol.3, 1933 - 1946. Cyril N. Barclay, London, 1950.

The Cameronians. Wolmer Whyte, 1941.

A short history of the Cameronians (Scottish Rifles). H.C. Wylly, Aldershot, 1925.

The Cameronians (Scottish Rifles); the story of a regiment. Douglas Ferrier, Glasgow, 1919.

Thomas Carter and a manuscript history of the 26th (or Cameronian) Regiment. Thomas Taylor, died 1836, ed. by Stephen Wood, in J. Soc. Army Hist. Res. vol. 65, 1987.

5th Battalion ' the Cameronians' (Scottish Rifles), 1914 - 1919. Glasgow, 1936.

7th Battalion the Cameronians (Scottish Rifles). ..... with the British Liberation Army in Europe. n.d., n.p.

10th Battalion the Cameronians (Scottish Rifles), 1914 - 1918. Edinburgh, 1923.

Soldiers died in the Great War, 1914 - 1919, part 31. H.M.S.O., 1921.

COLDSTREAM GUARDS

Coldstream Guards, 1885 - 1918. 5 vols. G.Davies, Sir J. Hall & Sir J. Ross-of-Bladensburg, 1924 - 1929.

FENCIBLES

The Northern or Gordon Fencibles, 1778 - 1783. [Inverness, Moray, Nairn]. H.B. Mackintosh, Edinburgh, 1929.

The Grant, Strathspey or First Highland Fencible Regiment, 1793 - 1799. H.B. Mackintosh, Elgin, 1934.

The Reay Fencibles, or Lord Reay's Highlanders. John MacKay, Glasgow, 1890.

An old Highland Fencible corps: the history of the Reay Fencible Highland Regiment of Foot, or Mackay's Highlanders, 1794 - 1802. I.H. Mackay Scobie, Edinburgh, 1914.

GORDON HIGHLANDERS

The History of the Gordon Highlanders, 1794 - 1898. [including an account of the 75th regiment, 1787 - 1898]. 2 vols., C. Greenhill Gardyne, London, Medici Society, 1929.

The Gordon Highlanders, 1919 - 1945. [The Life of a Regiment]. Wilfred Miles, Aberdeen Univ. Press, 1961.

Gordon Highlanders: muster roll at the period of Waterloo. J.M. Bulloch, Aberdeen, 1927.

Gordon Highlanders wounded at Waterloo. J.M. Bulloch, Aberdeen, 1916.

With the Gordons at Ypres. A.M. Maclean, 1916.

The Gordon Highlanders, Loos, Buzancy. Alick Buchanan Smith, Aberdeen, 1981.

Historical diary of the Gordon Highlanders. F.H. Neish, 1914.

The Gordon Highlanders: a short record of the services of the regiment. P.D. Thomson, Devonport, 1916.

The Gordon Highlanders, 2nd Battalion, as quartered at Banff, 1811 - 1812. J.M. Bulloch, Aberdeen, 1916.

4th Battalion Gordon Highlanders. R.A. Leitch, Tunbridge Wells, 1920.

6th Gordons in France & Flanders with 7th & 15th Scottish Divisions. D. Cullen MacKenzie, Aberdeen, 1921.

11th Battalion Gordon Highlanders, 1914 - 1916. Henry Alford, 1916.

Students Under Arms. History of Aberdeen University Company of Gordon Highlanders, 1914 - 1918. Alexander Rule, Aberdeen, 1934.

Soldiers died in the Great War, 1914 - 1919, part 65, Gordon
   Highlanders.   H.M.S.O., 1921.

HIGHLAND BRIGADE

The Highland Brigade. J. Cromb, Edinburgh, 1886.

HIGHLAND EMIGRANT REGIMENT

Scottish Highlanders and the American Revolution. G.   Murray
   Logan, Halifax, Nova Scotia, 1976.

HIGHLAND LIGHT INFANTRY

Historical   Records   of   the   71st Regiment,   Highland Light
   Infantry, 1777 - 1852. Richard Cannon, 1852.

Proud Heritage: the story of the Highland   Light   Infantry.
   L.B. Oatts, 1952.

Concise   Official History of the 2nd Battalion.   The Glasgow
   Highland Light Infantry.   Lübeck, Germany.

5 th Battalion Highland Light Infantry in the   war,   1914   -
   1918. n.p., 1921.

Highland Light Infantry,   - The Story of the 10th Battalion,
   1944 - 1945. R.T. Johnston, n.d., n.p..

An epic of   Glasgow;   history   of   the   15th   battalion   the
   Highland   Light   Infantry.   Thomas Chalmers,   Glasgow,
   1934.

History of the 16th H.L.I.;   a saga   of   Scotland.   Thomas
   Chalmers, Glasgow, 1930.

INVERNESS-SHIRE HIGHLANDERS

"The Inverness-shire Highlanders" or   97th regiment of foot,
   1794 - 1796. H.B. Mackintosh, Elgin, 1926.

LIVERPOOL SCOTTISH

The Liverpool Scottish, 1900 - 1919. A.M. Gilchrist, 1930.

LONDON SCOTTISH

The   London   Scottish in the second World War,   1939 - 1945.
   C.N. Barclay, London, 1952.

Cannon fodder: an infantryman's life on the Western Front, 1914 -1918.[London Scottish Regiment]. A. Stuart Dolden, Poole, 1908.

LORD OGILVY'S REGIMENT

The Muster Role of the Forfarshire or Lord Ogilvy's Regiment, raised on behalf of the Royal House of Stuart in 1745 - 1746. Alexander Mackintosh, Inverness, 1914.

LOVAT SCOUTS

The Story of the Lovat Scouts, 1900 - 1980. Michael Leslie Melville, Edinburgh, 1981.

MACKAY'S REGIMENT

"An Old Scots Brigade" being the History of Mackay's regiment. John Mackay, Edinburgh, 1885.

QUEEN'S OWN HIGHLANDERS

"Cuidich 'n righ": a history of the Queen's Own Highlanders (Seaforth & Camerons). Angus Fairrie, Inverness, 1983.

RATTRAY'S SIKHS

The Regimental History of the 45th Ratrray's Sikhs. vol.1, 1856 - 1914. H. St. G. M. McRae, Glasgow, 1933.

ROYAL ARTILLERY

The Scottish Horse, 1939 - 1945. The history of the 79th & 80th medium regiments of artillery. Glasgow, n.d

The 126th (Highland) Field Regiment R.A. in action, 1942 - 1945. Arbroath, 1946.

The City of Aberdeen Royal Field Artillery 157th brigade; a story of its raising. James Smith, Aberdeen Daily Journal, 1918.

ROYAL CORPS OF TRANSPORT

The Royal Corps of Transport. Golspie, c. 1981.

ROYAL SCOTS

The Royal Scots, 1914 - 1919. John Ewing, 1925.

The Regimental Records of the Royal Scots. J.C. Leask & H.M. McCance, 1915.

The Royal Scots (the Royal Regiment): Her Majesty's First
Regiment of Foot. Derby, 1980.

The Story of the Royal Scots (The Lothian Regiment)
Lawrence Weaver, n.d.

History of the Royal Scots. T.B. Simon, Edinburgh, 1943.

Lads of the Lothians; with the Royal Scots in Gallipoli.
Escott Lynn, 1920.

Freemasonry in the Royal Scots. T.R. Henderson, Aldershot,
1934.

The Leather Sporran. Journal of the Highlanders, The Royal
Scots, nos. 1 - 3, Edinburgh, 1916 - 1917.

Selections from the Inchkeith Lyre, the non official organ
of the 6th Battalion, the Royal Scots. ed. J.C.
Stewart, Edinburgh, 1920.

8th Royal Scots. Minor Tactics for non commissioned
officers. Edward Peterkin, 1897.

The Royal Scots:- Record of the 9th (volunteer) Battalion
of Highlanders, 1900-1909. James Ferguson, London,
1909.

ROYAL SCOTS FUSILIERS

Historical Record & Regimental Memoir of the Royal Scots
Fusiliers, formerly known as the 21st Royal North
British Fusiliers. James Clarke, 1885.

The History of the Royal Scots Fusiliers, 1678 - 1918. John
Buchan, London, 1925.

A field force in South Africa 1851. Michael Barthorp, in J.
Soc. Army Hist. Res., vol. 64, 1986.

The Royal Highland Fusiliers. Embodying the 21st fusiliers
(RSF) & the 71st & 74th Highlanders (HLI). Glasgow, c.
1962.

An' it's called a Tam-o'-Shanter. [Royal Scots Fusiliers].
Kenneth J. West, 1985.

Soldiers died in the Great War, 1914 - 1919, part 26, Royal
Scots Fusiliers. H.M.S.O., 1921.

THE ROYAL SCOTS GREYS

History of the 2nd Dragons - The Royal Scots Greys. Percy
Groves, London, 1893.

History of the 2nd Dragoons Royal Scots Greys. Edward
Almack, London, 1908.

History of the Royal Scots Greys, 1914 - 1919. R. Pomery,
London, 1928.

SCOTS GUARDS

Scots Guards; a memoir. Henry Dundas, 1921.

Scots Guards. Scotland's own Regiment of foot guards. n.d.

Scots Guard. Wifred Ewart, 1934.

The history of the Scots Guards from the creation of the regiment to the eve of the Great War. 2 vols.. Sir F. Maurice, 1935.

The Scots Guards in the Great War. F. Loraine Petre, 1925.

SCOTTISH HORSE

The Scottish Horse, 1900 - 1956. R.M.T. Campbell-Preston, Dunkeld, 1982 ?

SEAFORTH HIGHLANDERS

The Seaforth Highlanders, August 1914 - April 1916. H.H.E. Craster, Scottish Historical Review, vol. 16.

Seaforth Highlanders; photographs and short records of services of some of the senior officers of the S.H. (Ross-shire Buffs, the Duke of Albany's), 1793 - 1925. Edinburgh, 1926.

The 78th Highlanders (Ross-shire Buffs). Bill Crowell, Yarmouth, Nova Scotia, 1986.

Long way round: an escape through occupied France. William Moore, London, 1986.

Betting Book of the 2nd Battalion (78th) Seaforth Highlanders, 1822 - 1908. Privately printed, 1909.

A History of the 4th battalion, the Seaforth Highlanders with an account of the military annals of Ross, the fencibles and volunteers and reserve battalions, 1914 - 1919. M.M. Haldane, London, 1927.

"Sans Peur". The Seaforth Highlanders: history of the 5th Caithness & Sutherland Battalion, 1942 - 1945. A. Borthwick, Stirling, 1946.

War Diary of the 5th Seaforth Highlanders, 51st Highland Division. D. Sutherland, 1920.

10th Battalion Seaforth Highlanders in the Great War. Chilton L.A. Smith, 1927.

Soldiers died in the Great War, 1914 - 1919, part 64, the Seaforth Highlanders. H.M.S.O., 1921

9TH SCOTTISH DIVISION

Three years with the 9th (Scottish) Division. W.D. Croft, 1919.

History of the 9th (Scottish) Division, 1914 - 1919. J. Ewing, 1921.

9th (Scottish) Division Memorial, Arras, April 9, 1922. Ian Hay, 1922.

Year Book of the 9th Scottish Division. annually, London.

15TH SCOTTISH DIVISION

The History of the 15th Scottish Division, 1939 - 1945. H.G. Martin, Edinburgh, 1948.

The 15th (Scottish) Division, 1914 - 1919. J. Stewart & J. Buchan, 1926.

Scottish Corridor [Scottish 15th Division]. John Keegan, in Six Armies in Normandy, London, 1982.

51st HIGHLAND DIVISION

The History of the 51st (Highland) Division, 1914 - 1918. F.W. Brewsher, 1921.

51st Highland Division in Africa & Sicily. J. Borthwick, 1945.

The 51st Highland Division. Fred. A. Farrell, 1920.

The Highland Division. Eric Linklater, H.M.S.O., 1942.

The 51st Highland Division in France, 1914 - 1918. Robert B. Ross, London, 1918.

The History of the 51st Highland Division, 1939 - 1945. J.B. Salmond, Edinburgh, 1953.

51st Edinburgh Regiment. Standing Orders issued by Col., Earl of Ancram, 1812.

A medico's luck in the war; reminiscences of R.A.M.C. work with the 51st (Highland) Division. David Rorie, 1929.

52nd LOWLAND DIVISION

The mountain & the flood; the history of the 52nd (Lowland) Division, 1939 - 1946. George Blake, Glasgow, 1950.

The 52nd (Lowland) Division, 1914 - 1918. R.R. Thomson, 1923.

ENGINEERS

History of the Corps of Royal Engineers. 3 vols. W. Porter &
Sir Charles Watson, 1889 & 1915.

104 (City of Edinburgh) Field Squadron R.E., a history,
1859 - 1977. D. MacNiven, Edinburgh, 1979.

MILITIA

General

List of the Officers & of several Regiments & Corps of
militia & Fencibles raised since 1793. Also gentlemen
yeomanry & volunteer corps. London, 1794 - 1825 & 1917,
1918.

Edinburgh

The Edinburgh Militia of 1799. David Dobson, Scottish
Genealogist, vol.31, 1984.

MUSTER ROLLS

The Muster Roll of Angus, South African War, 1899 - 1900.
J.B. Salmond, Arbroath, 1900.

Muster roll of troops of horsemen, 1667. Charles Dalton, in
'Scots Army', 1909.

Muster rolls of the Earl of Mar's Regiment of Foot, 1683 -
1683. Charles Dalton, in 'Scots Army', 1909.

Muster Roll of Prince Charles Edward Stuart's Army, 1745 -
1746. Christian W.H. Aikman, Alastair Livingstone,
Betty Stuart Hart, Aberdeen University Press, 1984.

TERRITORIALS

Youth of Yesteryear: campaigns, battles, services and
exploits of the Glasgow Territorials in the last Great
War. Ion S. Munro, 1939.

The Glasgow Territorials: 52nd (Lowland) Division, 1888 -
1946; no. 602 (City of Glasgow) (Fighter) Squadron.
William P. Paul, Glasgow, 1946.

VOLUNTEERS

General

List of the Officers & of several Regiments & Corps of
militia & Fencibles raised since 1793. Also gentlemen
yeomanry & volunteer corps. London, 1794 - 1825 & 1917,
1918.

Volunteers of Great Britain. House of Commons, 1803.

Returns of the House of Commons Volunteer Corps, 1806.

Records of the Scottish and Volunteer Force, 1859 - 1908. J.M. Grierson, Edinburgh, 1909.

The Volunteer Artillery, 1859 - 1908. Norman E.H. Litchfield, Nottingham, 1982.

Volunteer Corps - Scottish regiments. Alasdair Maclean, Scots Mag. vol. 126, no.5, 1987.

History of the Aberdeen Volunteers. An account of the early volunteers of the counties of Aberdeen, Banff and Kincardine. Donald Sinclair, Aberdeen, 1907.

The Caithness Volunteers. D.K. Murray & E.G. Buik, Wick, 1907.

Roll of officers Dumbartonshire Volunteer Rifke Corps, 1860 - 1908, 9th battalion Argyll & Sutherland Highlanders, 1908 - 1920, 1st & 3rd volunteer battalions A & S Highlanders 1916 - 1920. F. Rorke, Dumbarton, 1920.

Forfarshire Artillery Volunteers. William Young Carman and J. Craig, in J. Soc. Army Hist. vol. 54, 1976.

Glasgow & Lanarkshire Volunteer Corps, 1804 - 1806. Philip J. Haythornthwaite, in Dispatch, no. 90, 1979.

List of the Loyal Greenock Volunteers, 1794. In 'Old Greenock', G. Williamson, 1886.

The Hawick Military Association, or first company of Hawick Volunteers, 1798 - 1802. J.J. Vernon, Trans. Hawick Arch. Soc., Hawick, 1901.

The Kincardineshire Volunteers from 1798 - 1816. William Will, Aberdeen, 1920.

5th Kirkcudbright Rifle Volunteers. James B. Mackay, in Dispatch, 1977.

History of the 7th Lanarkshire Rifle Volunteers. James Orr, 1884.

Lanarkshire Rifle Volunteers, 78th. Brian J. Hayton. in J. Soc. Army Hist. Res., vol. 59, 1981.

List of Corps of the Loyal Stirling Volunteers, 1800 - 1804. W.B. Cook, The Stirling Antiquary, 1904.

PRISONERS

Rebel Prisoners transported to Virginia, 1715. Scottish Notes & Queries, 3rd ser., no.4.

The prisoners of the '45. 3 vols. Sir Bruce Gordon Seton & Jean Gordon Arnot, Scottish History Society, 1929.

Rebel prisoners in Edinburgh, 1746. The Scottish Antiquary,
vi, p.127.

An exact list and description of 150 rebel prisoners ship'd
at Liverpool ... for the Leeward Islands. In 'Jacobite
Gleanings'. J. MacBeth Forbes, 1903.

List of 68 rebels from York Prison sailing for America.
1747. in 'Jacobite Gleanings', J. MacBeth Forbes, 1903.

NAVY

The Naval List, 1747 - 1991.

Biographia Navalis. Memoirs of officers of the Royal Navy
from 1600 - 1797. 6 vols. John Charnock, 1794 - 1798.

Naval Biographies, 1823 - 1835. 4 vols. Supplement, 4 vols.,
1827 - 1830. John Marshall, London.

The Naval biography of Great Britain, 4 vols. . James Ralfe,
1828.

Naval Biographical Dictionary. William R. O'Byrne, London,
1849. enlarged edition, 1861. [only published up to
H.S.G. Giles].

Commissioned Sea Officers of the Royal Navy. 3 vols.
National Maritime Museum, 1954.

Naval Honours & Awards, 1939 - 1959. Seedie, 1989.

The Royal Naval Medical Service. Christopher Lloyd & Jack
Leonard Saga Coulter, 1954.

A bibliography of British Naval History; a biographical &
historical guide to printed & manuscript sources. G.E.
Mainwaring, 1930.

Scots in the Russian Navy. Scottish Notes & Queries, 2nd.
ser. iii, 5.

MEDALS & AWARDS

General

The War Medal Record. 2 vols., Spink, London, 1896

The three great retrospective medals, 1793 - 1840, awarded
to artillery men. D.D. Vigors & A.M. Macfarlane, n.d.

Peninsular Medal Roll, 1793 - 1814. A.J. Newnham,
Portsmouth. [typescript - Scottish United Services
Museum Library].

Waterloo Medal Roll. London, 1984.

Catalogue of British, Hanoverian & other Waterloo Medals.
Kynaston Gaskell, London, 1905.

The Military General Service Medal, 1793 - 1814. K.O.N. Foster, 1947.

D.C.M.

Recipients of the DCM, 1914 - 1920. R.W. Walker, Birmingham, 1981.

Recipients of the DCM, 1855 - 1909. P.E. Abbot, London, 1975.

DCM citations, 1914 - 1920, 17 vols. London, n.d.

D.S.M.

The DSM, 1914 - 1920. W.H. Fevyer, Suffolk, 1982.

The DSM, 1939 - 1940. W.H. Fevyer, Suffolk, 1981.

G.C.

Register of the George Cross. Cheltenham, 1985.

G.M.

The George Medal. W.H. Fevyer, Spink, London, 1980.

Dragons can be defeated. [Record of the George Medal, 1940 - 1983]. D.V. Henderson, Spink, London, 1984.

M.C.

The Military Cross awarded to officers, 1939 - 1959. R.M. Kamaryc, Harlow, n.d.

O.B.E.

Handbook of the most excellent Order of the British Empire, 1921. ed. A. Winton Thorpe, London, 1988.

V.C. & D.S.O.

The Victoria Cross & Distinguished Service Order, 1856 - 1919, 3 vols. ed. Sir O'Moore Creagh & E.M. Humphris, London, n.d.

Naval

Naval General Service Medal, 1793 - 1840. Kenneth Douglas-Morris, London, 1982.

Naval General Service Medal Roll, 1793 - 1840. A.J. Newnham, [typescript Scottish United Services Museum Library].

Naval Medals, 1793 - 1856. Kenneth Douglas-Morris, London, 1987.

Airforce

The Meritorious Service Medal to Aerial Forces. Ian McInnes, Chippenham, 1984.

Canada

The Military Medal, Canadian Recipients, 1916 - 1922. Harry & Cindy Abbnik, Calgary, 1987.

Canada General Service Roll, 1866 - 1870. G.A. Brown, 1983.

China

The China War Medal, 1900, to the Royal Navy & Royal Marines. W.H. Fevyer, London, 1985.

India

The Army of India Medal Roll, 1799 - 1826. R.W. Gould, London, 1974.

Early Indian Campaigns & Decorations, 1780 - 1859. H. Biddulph, n.d.

South Africa

South African War Honours & Awards, 1899 - 1902. 1903, reprint, 1987.

The South African 1853 Medal. G.R. Everson, London, 1978.

Boer War Tribute Medals. M.G. Hibbard, London, 1982.

The Queen's South Africa Medal to the Royal Navy & Royal Marines. W.H. Fevyer & J.W. Wilson, Spink, London, 1983.

ROLLS OF HONOUR

[and casualty lists]
[See under SCHOLARS & STUDENTS also].

General

Their Name Liveth for Ever More. The Book of the Scottish National War Memorial. Ian Hay, London, 1931.

The Roll of Honour. H.M. Naval & Military Forces who fell in the Great War. 74 volumes, London.

Bond of Sacrifice. Biographical Record of Officers who fell in the Great War. 2 vols. Aug. 1914 - June 1915. ed. L.A. Clutterbuck, London, 1916.

War Graves of the British Empire. London, 1931.

Clan Donald Roll of Honour, 1914 - 1918. Glasgow, 1931.

Clan Mackay War Memorial, deaths & honours. Glasgow, 1924.

Clan Macrae Roll of Honour & Service in the Great War. Elle
    Macrae-Gilstrap, Aberdeen, 1925.

Muster Roll of the Manse, 1914 - 1919. ed. Duncan Cameron,
    1919.

Roll of Honour of Members of the Writers to the Signet, 1914
    - 1919. Edinburgh, n.d.

The Inns of Court Officers Training Corps in the Great War.
    F.H.L. Errington, London, n.d.

Stonyhurst War Record. Francis Irwin, 1927.

Casualty Lists

Second Afghan War, 1878 - 1880 Casualty Roll.   Anthony
    Farrington, London, 1986.

Casualty Roll for the Crimea. Frank & Andrea Cook, London,
    1976.

Casualty Roll for the Indian Mutiny, 1857 - 1859. I.T.
    Tavender, Suffolk, 1983.

The South African War Casualty Roll. 2 vols. Suffolk, 1982.

Casualty Roll for the Zulu & Basuto Wars, South Africa, 1877
    - 1879. I.T. Tavender, Suffolk, 1985.

Aberdeenshire

The War Book of Turriff & 12 miles round, 1914 - 1919. Roll
    of honour of the area. J. Minto Robertson, Turriff,
    1926.

Aberdeen University Roll of Service in the Great War, 1914
    - 1919. ed. Mabel Desborough Allardyce, Aberdeen Univ.
    Press, 1921.

The North of Scotland Bank Ltd. War Record, 1914 - 1918.
    Aberdeen, 1925.

Angus

Roll of Honour Arbroath & District, 1939 - 1945. T. Buncle,
    Arbroath, n.d.

Forfar & District in the War. A record of service in the
    great struggle, 1914 - 1919. D.M. Mackie, 1921.

Banffshire

Roll of Honour 1914 - 1919 for the town and parish of
    Macduff, Banffshire. George Forbes Dickson, Banff,
    1919.

Coatbridge

Coatbridge & the Great War. Samuel Lindsay, Glasgow, 1919.

Greenock

Men of Greenock who fell in the Great War. Greenock, n.d.

Kilmalcolm

Parish of Kilmalcolm Roll of Service, 1914 - 1918. n.p., n.d.

Lewis

Island of Lewis Roll of Honour, 1914 - 1918. Stornoway, 1920.

Loch Broom

Records of the men of Loch Broom, 1914 - 1918. Mrs. Fraser, Glasgow, 1922.

Peebleshire

Peebleshire Roll of Honour [men enrolled August 1914 - December 1915]. Peebles, 1916.

Perthshire

Golden Book. Perth & Perthshire Roll of Honour. Perth, 1928.

Selkirkshire

Roll of Honour of 1296 men from the burgh and parish of Selkirk who served in the great war, 1914 - 1918. Edinburgh, 1921.

Shetland

Shetland's Roll of Service. Lerwick, 1915

Shetland's Roll of honour and roll of service. Thomas Manson, Lerwick, 1920.

Tweedale

Book of Rememberance for Tweedale. 5 vols. ed Dr. Gunn, Peebles, 1920 - 1925.

YEOMANRY

General

List of the Officers & of several Regiments & Corps of militia & Fencibles raised since 1793. Also gentlemen yeomanry & volunteer corps. London, 1794 - 1825 & 1917, 1918.

A short history of the Ayrshire Yeomanry, 151st Field Regiment, 1939 - 1946. I.A. Graham Young, Ayr, 1947.

A History of the Ayrshire Yeomanry Cavalry. W.S. Cooper, Edinburgh, 1881.

Historical Records of the Border Yeomanry Regiments. B.F.M. Freeman, Kelso, 1906.

The Fife & Forfar Yeomanry, and 14th battalion, R.H. ,1914 - 1919. D.D. Ogilvie, London, 1921.

Fife & Forfar Imperial Yeomanry and its predecessors. G. Bourgoyne, Fife, 1904.

Queen's Own Royal Glasgow Yeomanry, 1848 - 1948. Glasgow, 1948.

The Old Kirkcudbright Yeomanry. J. Robison in The Gallovidian, winter, 1913.

A short account of the first Lothians and Border Yeomanry in the campaign of 1940 and 1944 - 1945. W.A. Woolward, Edinburgh, 1946.

The Stirlingshire Yeomanry Cavalry and the Scottish radical disturbances of April 1820. P.J.R. Mileham, in Journal of Scottish Army History Research, vol. 63 & 64, 1985.

List of the Strathhendrick Yeomanry. The Stirling Antiquary, 1908.

UNIFORMS

Scottish Military Dress. Peter Cochrane, London, 1987.

The uniforms and History of the Scottish Regiments, from 1660 to the present. R.M. Barnes, 1956.

A history of the regiments and uniforms of the British Army. R.M. Barnes, 1950.

The Scottish Troops. Liliane & Fred Funcken, in their British Infantry Uniforms: from Marlborough to Wellington. London, 1976.

The uniforms of the Royal Scots Dragoon Guards (Carabiniers & Greys). R.B. Anderson, in J. Soc. Army Hist. Res. vol. 56, 1979.

The 71st Highland Light Infantry, 1834 - 1839. J.B. McKay. in Dispatch, no.90, 1979.

Badges of the Highland and Lowland Regiments, (including volunteer & territorial battalions). William H. & K.D. Bloomer, London, c. 1982.

Scottish Regimental Badges, 1793 - 1971. Wiliiam H. & K.D. Bloomer, London, 1982.

Richard Simkin's Uniforms of the British Army. W.Y. Carman, Exeter, 1985.

PENSIONERS

Pensioners Index, 66th-73rd Foot, 1806-1838. J.D. Beckett, n.d.

Pensioners Index, 74th-82nd Foot. J.D.Beckett, n.d.

INDIA

Alphabetical List of officers in the Indian Army, 1760 - 1834. Edward Dodwell, London, 1838.

Officers of the Bengal Army, 1758 - 1834. 4 vols. V.C.P. Hodson, London, 1926 - 1946.

List of Officers, Bombay Artillery, from 1749. Col. F.W.M. Spring, London, 1902.

****

MILLINERS

Edinburgh

The Edinburgh Milliners, 1720-1820. Elizabeth Sanderson, in Costume, no. 20, 1986.

MISSIONARIES

A Pioneering Ministry: Presbyterian Home Missionaries in New Zealand, 1862-1964. Harold Scott, Wellington, 1983.

Christian Doctor & Nurse: the History of the Medical Missions in South Africa from 1799-1976. Michael Gelfand, 1984.

Scottish Free Church Missionary Society. J. Kofi Agbeti, in West African Church History, Leiden, 1986.

Register of Missionaries & Deputations, 1796-1877. John Owen Whitehouse, London, 1877.

MONARCHS

Scotland's kings and queens. Alan Bold, London, c.1980.

Kings & Kingship in Early Scotland. M.O. Anderson, Edinburgh, 1980.

Scottish Kings. 1005-1625. Archibald Dunbar, Edinburgh, 1906.

The Scots Compendium or Rudiments of Honour. The succession of Scots Kings from Fergus. 5th ed. London, 1752.

MUSICIANS

General   [see Entertainers also].

The Royal Society of Musicians of Great Britain list of
    Members, 1738 - 1984. Betty Matthews, London, 1985.

Grove's Dictionary of Musicians. 5th edn. 9vols. ed. by Eric
    Blom, London, 1954. Supplement, 1961.

Scottish Women Composers. John Purser. In Chapman, 27/28,
    1980.

The Genealogy of early Scottish music & composers. Kenneth
    Elliott, Scottish Genealogist, vol.3, no.3, 1956.

The Musical Directory, Annual and Almanac. [1855 - 1931].

Reeve's Musical Directory. [1879 - 1902].

The Music Trades Pocket Directory. [1888 - 1898].

Music Trade Directory. [1916 - 1939].

Music Industries Directory. [1925 - 1929].

Aberdeen

Precentors and musical professors. W. Anderson, Aberdeen,
    1876.

University Sacrists. [holders 16th - 20th centuries]. C.B.R.
    Butchart, in Aberd. Univ. Rev. vol. 41, 65-70.

Glasgow

The history of the Glasgow Society of Musicians, 1884-1944.
    E.J.V. Brown, 1947.

Wind Instruments

An index of wind instrument makers. Lyndesay Graham
    Langwill, Edinburgh 1977.

Stringed Instruments

Scottish Violin Makers: past & present. William C. Honeyman,
    1984 reprint of 1910 edition, Richmond, Va.

Strathspey Players past and present. William C. Honeyman.
    Edinburgh, 1984.

Scottish Violin Makers. Wm. C. Honeyman. Rep. Bridgwater,
    1981.

PAPER-MAKING

The Expansion of the British Paper Industry, 1860-1914,
    particularly in Scotland. J.N.Bartlett, London:
    Economic & Social Research Council, 1984 - microfiche.

The Paper making industry in Scotland. John C. B. Cooper, in Scott. Bankers' Mag., 1981.

Our ancient and honourable craft, 1750-1933. Alexander A. Cormack, London, 1933.

The Paper Industry in Scotland, 1590-1861. Alistair G. Thomson, Edinburgh, 1974.

The Paper Stainers Directory of Great Britain. [1874].

The Paper Mills Directory. [1860 - 1941].

Kelly's Directory of Stationers, Printers, Booksellers, Papermakers of England, Scotland, Wales & Ireland. [1872 - 1939].

Directory of Papermakers of the U.K. [1886 - 1950].

The Paper Trade Diary Directory. [1903 - 1949].

Aberdeen

Alexander Pirie & Sons. Aberdeen and the expansion of the British paper industry, c.1860-1914. J. Neville Bartlett, in Bus. Hist., vol.22, 1980.

Edinburgh

Early Paper making near Edinburgh. Robert Waterston, B.O.T.O.E.C., vols. 25,27,28, 1945, 1949, 1953.

PEDDLERS

From Packmen, Tallymen and "perambulating Scotchmen" to credit drapers' associations, c.1840-1914. Gerry R. Rubin, in Bus. Hist. vol. 28, 1986.

PEERS, NOBLES & ARMIGERS

The Peerage of Scotland. George Crawford, Edinburgh, 1716.

The Peerage of Scotland. Sir Robert Douglas. 2nd ed. John Philip Wood, 2 vols., Edinburgh, 1813.

The Scots Peerage, 9 vols.. Sir James Balfour Paul, Edinburgh, 1904 - 1914.

The Jacobite Peerage. Marquis of Ruvigny & Raineval, Edinburgh, 1904.

Burke's Peerage. John Burke (& various later editors), 1st ed. 1826 - 150th edition, 1970.

Burke's Extinct Peerage. John Burke, 1840, 1846, 1866 & 1883.

Burke's Extinct Baronetcies. 1838 & 1841.

Debrett's Peerage. 1769 - 1984.

The Complete Peerage, 13 vols. George Edward Cokayne, London, 1910 - 1940.

The Baronage of Scotland. Sir Robert Douglas, Edinburgh, 1798.

Burke's Landed Gentry. John Burke, 1833 - 1972 (18th edition).

Who Was Who. 7 vols., 1897 - 1980. London, 1920 - 1988.

Heraldry

A System of Heraldry, 2 vols. Alexander Nisbet, Edinburgh, 1722.

Scottish Arms, 2 vols. R.R.Stodart, Edinburgh, 1881.

Burke's General Armory. 1842 - 4th reprint of 1884 edition in 1969.

Armorial Families, 2 vols.. Arthur Charles Fox-Davies, London, 1929, 7th edition.

Fairbairn's Book of Crests, 2 vols.. Edinburgh, 1905. Reprinted Poole, 1986.

POETS

The Poets & Poetry of Scotland, 2 vols.. James Grant Wilson, London, 1877.

The poets & poetry of Scotland from James I to the present time. Andrew R. Bonar, Edinburgh, 1866.

The Leading poets of Scotland from early times. Walter J. Kaye, London, 1892.

Poets & Poetry of the Scottish Border. R. Murray, Trans. Hawick Arch. Soc., Hawick, 1867.

The Bards of Galloway. Malcolm Harper, Dalbeattie, 1889.

Scottish Poets recent and living. Alexander G. Murdoch, Glasgow, 1883.

Living Scottish Poets. C.M. Grieve, London, 1931.

Angus

Bards of Angus & the Mearns. A. Reid, 1897.

Ayrshire

The Poets of Ayrshire, from the 14th century to the present day. John MacIntosh, Dumfries, 1910.

Clackmannanshire

The Poets of Clackmannanshire. ed. J. Beveridge, Glasgow, 1885.

Galloway

The Bards of Galloway. Malcolm McL. Harper, Dalbeattie, 1889.

Linlithgowshire

The Poets & Poetry of Linlithgowshire. Alex M. Bisset, Paisley, 1896.

Yarrow

Yarrow: its poets & poetry. R. Borland, Dalbeattie, 1890.

POLICEMEN

Edinburgh

The Edinburgh Police Register, 1815 - 1859. Peter Ruthven-Murray, Edinburgh, 1991.

POLITICIANS & DIPLOMATS

Members of Parliament, Scotland ... 1357 - 1882, Joseph Foster, London, 1882.

The House of Commons, 1790 - 1820, 5 vols. [4 vols. of biographies]. R.G. Thorne, London, 1986.

The Parliaments of Scotland, Sir Robert Sangster Rait, Glasgow, 1924.

British Parliamentary Election Results, 1832 - 1973. 6 vols., F.W.S.Craig, Dartmouth, 1989.

A guide to the papers of British Cabinet Ministers, 1900 - 1951, Cameron Hazelhurst & Christine Woodland, London, 1974.

Private Papers of British Diplomats, 1782 - 1900. H.M.S.O., 1985.

Private papers of British Colonial Governors, 1782 - 1900. H.M.S.O., 1986.

Papers of British Politicians, 1782 - 1900. H.M.S.O., 1989.

Sources in British Political History, Chris Cook, London:
    v.1, 1975. Archives of selected organisations & societies.
    v.2, 1975. Private papers of selected public servants.
    v.3, 1977. Private papers of M.Ps., A - K.
    v.4, 1977. Private papers of M.Ps., L - Z.

v.5, 1978. Private papers of selected writers, intellectuals, publicists.
v.6, 1985. Supplement.

Dighton's Diplomatic Corps & Consular Directory. [1937].

Aberdeen

Notes on the members of Parliament for the burgh of Aberdeen, 1357-1866. A.M. Munro, Aberdeen, 1889.

Banffshire

Banffshire M.P.s since the Act of Union, A.N.Taylor & H. Taylor, Elgin, 1930.

Morayshire

Morayshire M.P.s since the Act of Union, A.N.Taylor & H. Taylor, Elgin 1930.

POTTERS & POTTERIES

Scottish East Coast Potteries, 1750-1840. Patrick McVeigh, Edinburgh, 1979.

Encyclopaedia of British Pottery & Porcelain Marks. Geoffrey A. Godden, London, 1964. [7th reprint 1986].

Scottish Pottery. J. Arnold Fleming, 1923.

Pottery Gazette & Glass Trade Review Directory. [1905 - 1967].

PRINTERS & BOOKSELLERS

General

Dictionary of Printers & Booksellers, 1726 - 1775. G.H.Bushnell, Oxford, 1932.

Scottish Printers & Booksellers, 1668 - 1775. A supplement, "Studies in Bibliography" XII, 1959, by R.H.Carnie and R.P.Doig.

A History of Scottish Bookbinding, 1432-1650. William Smith Mitchell, Edinburgh, 1955.

Printers & Publishers devices in England & Scotland 1485-1640. R. McKerrow. Bibliographical Society, 1949.

A Dictionary of Printers and Booksellers, 1668 - 1725. H.R.Plomer, Oxford, 1922.

Bookbinders Outside London, 1780 - 1840. Charles Ramsden, Tiptree, 1987. [reprint].

Books published abroad by Scotsmen before 1700. James H. Baxter, Records of the Glasgow Bibliographical Society, vol.11, 1933.

Catalogue of specimens of printing types by English & Scottish printers & founders, 1665-1830. W. Turner Berry & A.F. Johnson, Oxford Univ. Press, 1935.

Copyright in Scotland before 1709. William J. Couper, Records of the Glasgow Bibliographical Society, vol.9, 1931.

Scottish-American bookbindings. Hannah D. French, in Bookbinding in Early America, Worcester, Mass., 1986.

The small publisher: a manual & case histories. Audrey Ward, Cambridge, 1979.

The Revival of Scottish Publishing. Norman Wilson, in Crann-tara, no.9 1979/1980.

Quaker Printers, 1750-1850, R.S. Mortimer, in Journal of the friends Hist. Soc. vol 1., 100-133.

Hodson's Booksellers, Publishers & Stationers Directory for London & Country. [1855].

Kelly's Directory of Stationers, Printers, Booksellers and Papermakers of England, Scotland, Wales & Ireland. [1872 - 1939].

Clegg's Directory of Booksellers. [1888 - 1950].

The Bookman Directory of booksellers, publishers and authors. [1893].

The Direcotry of secondhand booksellers. [1886].

Directory of Antiquarian booksellers. [1921, 1927, 1932].

Aberdeen

Aberdeen Printing Presses On. in Leopard, 1976.

Aberdeen Master Printers' Guild. Record of the celebration of the tercentenary of the introduction of the art of printing into Aberdeen by Edward Raban in 1622. Aberdeen, 1923.

The Aberdeen Printers: Edward Raban to James Nicol. 1884.

Ayrshire

Printing in Ayr & Kilmarnock, c.1780-1920. Carreen S. Gardner, in Ayr Collect., vol.12, 1976.

Dumfries

Dumfries Printers in the 18th Century, with handlists of their marks. George W. Shirley, Dumfries, 1934.

Edinburgh

Wills of Printers & Booksellers in Edinburgh, 1627 - 1687. Bannantyne Club miscellany no.2, 1836.

The Edinburgh Society's silver medals for printing. Brian Hillyard, in Pap. Bibliogr. Soc. Am., vol.78, 1984.

Britannica's typesetters women compositors, in Edinburgh. Ed. Sian Reynolds, Edinburgh Univ. Press, 1989.

Fife

The Tullis Press, Cupar, 1803-1849. D.W.Doughty. Abertay Society Publication no.12, 1967.

Inverness

Old Inverness Booksellers. William Simpson, Inverness, 1931.

Kilmarnock

Kilmarnock Printing in the 18th century. W.T. Johnston, Edinburgh, 1982.

See also Ayrshire.

Perth

Publishing in Perth. [A list of Stationers, booksellers, bookbinders and printers, 1591 - 1807.] R.H.Carnie, Abertay Scoiety publication no.6, 1960.

Shetland

500 years of printing - 114 in Shetland. Thomas Mortimer Yule Manson, Shetland Times, 1976.

Newspapers

Directory of Scottish Newspapers. J.P.S. Ferguson, Edinburgh, 1984.

Documents relative to the printers of some early Scottish Newspapers, 1686-1705. Maitland Club Misc. vol.2, 1840.

Dalkeith

Dalkeith Advertiser Index, 1951 - 1954. [ms. at Roslin Library].

Dumfries & Galloway

Index of the Dumfries & Galloway Standard & Advertiser & its predecessors, 1777 - 1930. 8 vols., James Urquhart, Dumfries, 1980 - 1989.

Glasgow

Index to the Glasgow Herald , 1906 - 1978. Glasgow.

Midlothian

Midlothian Journal selective index, 1890. [ms. at Roslin library].

Stirling

Index to the Stirling Journal & Advertiser, 1820 - 1970; & Stirling Observer, 1836 - 1856. District Library, Stirling, & University of Stirling, 1978 - 1988.

England

Index to the Times. 1785 - 1989+. London.

PRISONERS

Prisoners of war in Britain, 1756-1815. F. Abell, Oxford, 1914.

PROFESSORS

Scottish University Professors, 1860-1939. R.D. Anderson, in Scottish Economic Social History, vol.7, 1987.

Portraits of the High Officers & Professors of the university of Edinburgh at its tercentenary festival. William Hole, Edinburgh, 1884.

PROSTITUTES

Directory of ladies of pleasure in Edinburgh. James Tytler ?, Edinburgh, 1775. reprint, Edinburgh, 1978.

PROVOSTS

Aberdeen

Memorials of the Aldermen, Provosts and Lord Provosts of Aberdeen, 1272-1895. A.M. Munro, Aberdeen, 1897.

Edinburgh

The Lord Provosts of Edinburgh, 1296 - 1932. Marguerite Wood for Sir Thomas Whitson, Edinburgh, 1932.

Glasgow

Biographical sketches of the Hon. Lord Provosts of Glasgow. Glasgow, 1883.

Lord Provosts of Glasgow, 1833 - 1902. Glasgow, 1902.

St. Andrews

The municipal relics of St. Andrews, and some of its early provosts. D.H.Fleming, St. Andrews, 1905.

RAILWAYMEN

Post Office Railway Directory for 1847 [chairmen, deputy-chairmen & directors].

The Railway Diary & Official Directory, 1922.

The Universal Directory of Railway Officials, 1895 - 1950.

SALT MAKERS

Scottish Salt making in the 18th century. Christopher Whatley, in Scott. Ind. Hist. vol.5, 1982.

An Early 18th century Scottish saltwork: Arran. Christopher Whatley, in Ind. Archaeol. Rev., vol.6, 1982.

Ayrshire

The Ayrshire Salt Industry, c.1707-1879. C. Whatley, in Scott. Industr. Hist., vol.1, 1977.

Prestonpans

Prestonpans: Scotland's last saltworks. Alex. Hamilton, Edinburgh, 1976.

SCHOLARS

General

History of the Burgh Schools of Scotland. James Grant, Glasgow, 1876.

Aberdeen

Aberdeen Grammar School, Roll of pupils 1795 - 1919. T.Wall, Aberdeen 1922.

Chanonry House School, Aberdeen, 'Spirat adhuc amor', a roll of old boys, 1849 - 1879. A.Shewan, Aberdeen 1923.

Dalkeith

List of eminent scholars educated at Dalkeith Grammar School. in Statistical Account of Edinburghshire, 1845, p. 493.

Dollar

Dollar Academy Roll of Honour, 1914 - 1919. circa 1932. [ms. in Scottish United Services Museum Library].

Dunfermline

Roll of Honour of Pupils and Staff of Dunfermline High School, 1914-1919. Dunfermline, 1920.

Edinburgh

Cargilfield Register, 1873 - 1927. Leith, 1928.

Edinburgh Academy Register: a record of all those who have entered the school since its foundation in 1824. Ed. T.Henderson & P.F. Hamilton-Grierson, Edinburgh, 1914.

The Edinburgh Academy: Prize List and annual report. Yearly from 1824.

The Edinburgh Academical Club Annual List.[names & addresses.]

War Supplement to Edinburgh Academy Register, Edinburgh 1921.

Edinburgh Academy War Service Record, 1939 - 1945. Edinburgh, 1949.

The Clacken & the Slate. (The story of Edinburgh Academy, 1824 - 1974). Magnus Magnusson, London, 1974.

The Fettes College Register 1870 - 1909. 4th edn. ed. M.J.C. Meiklejohn, Edinburgh 1909.

The Loretton Register 1825 - 1925. 2nd. edn., ed. A.H.Buchanan-Dunlop, Edinburgh 1927.

Edinburgh Institution 1832 - 1932, [Melville College]. Ed. J.R.S.Young, Edinburgh 1933.

Edinburgh High School: List of the gentlemen who attended Benjamin Mackay's class, 1839-1843. Edinburgh, 1868.

George Heriots School Roll of Honour, 1914 - 1919. Edinburgh, 1921.

Merchiston Castle School Register, 1833 - 1962, 5th edn. Ed. E.O.Connell, Edinburgh 1962.

Royal High School, roll of honour, 1914 - 1918. Edinburgh, 1920.

Royal High School, Roll of Honour, 1939 - 1945. Ed. W.C.A.Ross, Edinburgh, 1949.

St. George's School for Girls: Centenary Register, 1888-1988. [names, dates at school, addresses.]

The Watsonian War Record, 1939-1945. Watsonian Club, Edinburgh, 1951.

Glasgow

Glasgow Academy Roll of Honour, 1914-1918. G.H.R. Laird, Glasgow, 1933.

The High School of Glasgow, Book of Service & Rememberance. Frank Beaumont, Glasgow, 1921.

The Glasgow Academy, 1846 - 1946. Glasgow, 1946

Hawick

School Roll of the Hawick Academy, 1857-1864. Peter
Ruthven-Murray, Border F.H.S. Newsletter, 1988.

Inverness

The Inverness Academical War Memorial Number. Inverness,
1921.

Lanark

Lanark Grammar School, 1183-1983. A.D.Robertson & Thomas
Harvey, Lanark, 1983.

Musselburgh

List of the scholars educated by the late John Taylor at the
Grammar School of Musselburgh, from 1790 - 1820.
[Edinburgh Public Libraries].

Perthshire

The Glenalmond Register, 1847-1929. F.W.M., Edinburgh,1929.

A list of old Glemalmond's who served in the war, 1914 -
1919. Perth, 1919.

St. Andrews

St. Leonard's School Register, vol. 1 1877 - 1895; vol. 2
1895 - 1900. St. Andrews, 1895 & 1901.

SCIENTISTS

The manuscripts of British Scientists, 1600 - 1940.
H.M.S.O., 1982.

A Biographical dictionary of Scientists. Trevor I.
Williams, London, 1976.

British Association for the advancement of science. List of
members present at the meeting of September, 1834.

SEAMEN

Aberdeen

A short history of the Shipmasters' Society of Aberdeen,
formerly the Seamen's Box of Aberdeen, 1598-1911. A.
Clark, Aberdeen, 1911.

Shetland

Shetlanders in the Royal Navy in the time of the press gang.
Alan Beattie, in New Shetlander, nos. 150, 151, 152.
1984-1985.

SHIPOWNERS & SHIP BUILDERS

Directory of Shipowners, Shipbuilders and Marine Engineers.
[1903 - 1950].

SKINNERS

The Tanneries' Directory of England. [1867 - 1869].

Kelly's Directory of the Leather Trades. [1871 - 1940].

Records of British Industry, 1760 - 1914, Textiles &
Leather. H.M.S.O., 1990.

Edinburgh

The Incorporation of the Skinners of Edinburgh, 1549-1603.
William Angus, B.O.T.O.E.C., vol.6, 1913.

Glasgow

History of the Skinners, Furriers and Glovers of Glasgow.
Harry Lumsden, Glasgow, 1937.

Annals of the Skinners' Craft in Glasgow, 1516-1616. William
Whyte, Glasgow, 1875.

Stirling

The Incorporation of skinners of Stirling. David B. Morris,
Stirling, 1925.

SLATERS

Dundee

The 3 United Trades of Dundee: masons, wrights, slaters.
Annette M. Smith. Abertay Historical Society, 1987.

SMUGGLERS

A selected Bibliography on highwaymen, outlaws, pirates and
smugglers. Compiled R. Cameron, Mitchell Library, 1983.

Smugglers on the Solway. Scottish Genealogist, vol.31,
1984.

The Border Smugglers. R.Murray, Hwick Arch. Soc. Trans.,
Hawick, 1875.

The Solway Smugglers. Gordon Irving, Dumfries, 1971.

The Solway smugglers and the customs port at Dumfries.
W.A.J. Prevost, in Trans. Dumfries Galloway Nat. Hist.
Antiq. Soc., 3rd. ser. vol.51, 1975.

Smuggling in the Solway and around the Galloway seaboard. J.M. Wood, Dumfries, 1908.

The Smugglers. Duncan Fraser, Montrose, 1978.

Peterhead

The Peterhead smugglers of the last century. P.Buchan, Edinburgh, 1834.

SOAP MAKERS

The Soap Makers Directory of Great Britain. [1888 - 1955].

STUDENTS

General

Record of Fellows & Scholars and of teaching fellows of the Carnegie Trust for the Universities of Scotland, 1903-1905. J. Robb, Edinburgh, 1935.

Scottish Students in Heidelberg, 1386-1662. W. Caird Taylor, Scottish Historical Review, vol.5, 1908.

The Scottish Nation in the University of Orleans, ed. John Kirkpatrick, Scot. Hist. Soc. Misc. 1904.

Scottish Students at Louvain University. Scot. Hist. Rev. xxv. 329-334.

Index to English speaking students at Leyden University, 1575 - 1875. Edward Peacock, Index Society, 1884.

Registers of Students in the Scots Colleges at Douai, Rome, Madrid, Valladolid and Ratisbon, 1581 - 1900. New Spalding Club, Aberdeen, 1906.

The Scottish College at Douai, with a list of personnel, 1656 - 1760. J.H. Baxter, Scottish Historical Review, xxiv.

Les Etudiants Etrangers a l'universite de Paris au XV siecle, [some Scottish students] A.L. Gabriel in Annales de l'Universite de Paris, vol. 29, 377-400.

Scottish Students at Helmstedt University, 1585 - 1612. Scottish Historical Review, xxiv.

Aberdeen

Officers and Graduates of University and King's College, Aberdeen. Ed. P.J.Anderson. New Spalding Club, Aberdeen 1893.

Fasti Academiae Mariscallanae Aberdonensis, 1593 - 1860. P.J. Anderson & J.F.K. Johnstone. New Spalding Club, 3 volumes: - 4,18,19.

Roll of Graduates of the University of Aberdeen, 1860-1900. W. Johnston, Aberdeen University Studies, Aberdeen, 1900.

Roll of Alumni in Arts of the University and King's College of Aberdeen, 1596 - 1860, P.J.Anderson, Aberdeen 1900.

Roll of the Graduates of the University of Aberdeen 1860 - 1900. W. Johnston, Aberdeen 1906: with Roll of Graduates 1901 - 1925; with supplement 1860 - 1900 compiled by Theodore Watt, Aberdeen 1935.

Aberdeen alumni at other universities, 1494-1911. 1. Oxford & Cambridge. Aberdeen University Studies, no.51, Aberdeen, 1911.

The Universities of Aberdeen. Sir Robert Sangster Rait. Aberdeen, 1895.

Class Records of the University exist from 1860 onwards.

Commissioners on Aberdeen Universities, 1716-1717. Aberdeen 1900.

Cambridge

Alumni Cantabrigiensis to 1900. 10 vols. J.A. Venn, Cambridge, 1922 - 1953.

Biographical Register of the University of Cambridge to 1500. A.B. Emden, Cambridge, 1963.

Edinburgh

A Catalogue of the Graduates in the Faculty of Arts, Divinity & Law of the Unviersity of Edinburgh since its Foundation, 1553-1858. Bannantyne Club, 1858.

Edinburgh University Calendar. Pub. James Thin, Edinburgh. [various years, e.g.1950, 1954].

The Story of the University of Edinburgh, during its first three hundred years. Alexander Grant, 1884.

Four centuries: Edinburgh University Life, 1583-1983. Gordon Donaldson, Edin. Univ. Press, 1983.

Edinburgh University. List of the graduates in medicine from 1705 - 1866. Edinburgh, 1866.

Roll of Honour of the University of Edinburgh, 1914 - 1918. Edinburgh, 1921.

Glasgow

The Matriculation Albums of the University of Glasgow, from 1728 - 1858. William Innes Addison, Glasgow 1913.

A Roll of Graduates of the University of Glasgow from 1727 - 1897. William Innes Addison, Glasgow 1898.

The Snell Exhibitions from the University of Glasgow to Balliol College, Oxford, [list of holders 1679 - 1900]. William Innes Addison, Glasgow 1901.

History of the University of Glasgow. James Coutts. Glasgow, 1909.

The University of Glasgow, 1451 - 1897. John Duncan Mackie, Glasgow 1954.

Munimenta Alme Universitatis Glasguensis. Maitland Club, 3 vols. plus index vol., 1854.

Glasgow University Roll of Honour, 1914 - 1919. Glasgow, 1922.

The Royal Technical College Glasgow. Sacrifice & Service in the Great War. 1919.

Oxford

Alumni Oxoniensis, 1500 - 1714. 4 vols. Joseph Foster, Oxford, 1891 - 1892.

Alumni Oxioniensis, 1715 - 1886. 4 vols. Joseph Foster, Oxford, 1888.

St. Andrews

Acta Facultatis Artium Universitatis Sanctiandree, 1413-1588. Ed. Annie I. Dunlop, Scottish History Society, 3rd ser. vol.55.

The Graduation Roll of the University of St. Andrews, ed. J. Maitland Anderson. Scot. Hist. Soc., 3rd S., vol.8, 1926.

The Matriculation Roll of the University of St. Andrews. Ed. J.M.Anderson. Scot. Hist. Soc., 3rd S., vol. 8, 1926.

St. Andrews University Calendar. [not official, but containing lists of principals, professors, chancellors, masters and bachelors.] St. Andrews, 1851, and other issues.

St. Andrews University Calendar. [official] annually from 1865.

Early records of the University of St. Andrews. J.M. Anderson, Scottish History Society, Edinburgh, 1926.

STOCKBROKERS

Ralph's Stock and Share Brokers Directory. [1851 - 1858].

The Country Stockbrokers Directory. [1875].

The Untied Kingdom Stock and Sharebrokers Directory. [1881 - 1940].

SURVEYORS & MAPMAKERS

Old Maps & Map-makers of Scotland. John E. Shearer,
Stirling, 1905.

Some Notable Surveyors and Mapmakers of the sixteenth,
seventeenth and eighteenth centuries, and their work.
Sir Herbert George Fordham, Cambridge U.P., 1929.

Tooley's Dictionary of Mapmakers. Ronald Vere Tooley, Tring,
1979, with 1982 supplement.

Dictionary of Land Surveyors & Local Cartographers of Great
Britain & Ireland, 1550 - 1850. Edited Peter Eden, 4
volumes, 1975 - 1979.

British maps & map makers. Edward Lynam, 1944.

Blower's Architects', Surveyors', Engineers' and Builders'
Directory. [1860].

A Diary and Directory for the use of Surveyors, Auctioneers,
Land and Estate Agents. [1888 - 1939].

The Architects and Surveyors Directory and Referendum &
Diary. [1907 - 1912].

TAILORS

Canongate

The Incorporation of the Tailors of the Canongate.
W.H.Marwick, B.O.T.O.E.C., vol.22, 1938.

Glasgow

Excerpts from the records of the Incorporation of Tailors of
Glasgow. Glasgow, 1872.

Rights & Privileges of the Incorporation of Tailors in
Glasgow. Glasgow, 1872.

Incorporation of Tailors in Glasgow. The Incorporation,
Glasgow, 1970.

Hawick

Two 18th Century Tailors [Hawick]. Stuart Maxwell, repr.
Hawick Arch. Soc. Trans. 1972.

TEACHERS

List of Schoolmasters teaching Latin in 1690. Ed. Donald J.
Withrington, Scottish History Society, 1965.

The life & times of the schoolmaster in Central Scotland in
the 17th & 18th centuries. Andrew Bain, Callendar Park
College of Education, 1977.

Scottish School Board Directory & Teachers Guide, with index, 1882, 1885.

Abercorn

Schoolmasters of Abercorn Parish, 1646 - 1872. Donald Whyte, Scottish Genealogist, volume 15, no.1, March 1968.

Aberdeen

Aberdeen Grammar School Masters & Undermasters. P.J.Anderson, Scottish N. & Q., xi, Aberdeen, 1898.

Ayr

The Presbytery of Ayr: its schools & schoolmasters, 1642 - 1746. J.J. Fowler, in Ayrshire Archaeological & Nat. Hist. Collections, vol. 6, 81-174.

Banffshire

The schools & schoolmasters of Banffshire. William Barclay, Banff, 1925.

Dumfries & Galloway

The Edinburgh High School of Other Days. (A group of Dumfries & Galloway Masters). J. Maxwell Wood in The Gallovidian, winter, 1913.

Edinburgh

Teachers in Edinburgh in the 18th century. Alexander Law, B.O.T.O.E.C., vol.32, 1966.

Memorials and history of the Royal High School, Edinburgh, with biographies of the leading masters. W.S. Dalgleish, Edinburgh, 1857.

Greenock

The Grammar School Teachers in Greenock, 1727 - 1847. G. Williamson, in Old Greenock, 1888.

Hawick

The old schools and schoolmasters of Hawick & Wilton. J.J.Vernon, Hawick Archaeological Society, 1902.

Houston

Houston Schoolmasters. Donald Whyte, Scottish Genealogist, vol.11, 1964.

Keith

Historical account of the schools and schoolmasters in the parish of Keith, 1631. J. Lawrence, Keith, 1907.

TEMPLARS

Scottish Middle Templars. C.E.A. Bedwell, Scottish Historical Review, vol.17, 1920.

Aberdeen

The Knights-Templars in and around Aberdeen. A.Walker, Aberdeen Phil. Soc. vol.2, Aberdeen, 1887.

TENANTS

Tynron & Penpont tenants, 1695. A.E. Truckell, in Trans. Dumfries & Galloway Nat. Hist. & Antiq. Soc., vol.36. [rent arrears on Queensberry estate].

TINPLATERS & TINPLATING

Chronology of the tinplate works of Great Britain. Edward Henry Brooke, Cardiff, 1944.

Appendix to chronology of the tinplate works of Great Britain, 1665-1949. Edward Henry Brooke, Cardiff, 1950.

TOBACCO & TOBACCONISTS

Kelly's Directory of the Grocery, Oil & Colour Trades, including Tobacco Trades of England, Wales & Scotland. [1872 - 1922].

The Archaeology of the clay tobacco pipe. Ed. Peter Davey, Oxford, 1987.

Dumfries & Galloway

Clay pipes from Dumfries & Galloway. James Williams, in The Archaeology of the Clay Pipe. III, Britain: the north west, edited Peter Davey, Oxford, 1980.

Dunfermline

Richmond & others, pipemakers, Dunfermline. Martin Horgate, in The Archaeology of the clay tobacco pipe. III Britain: the north and west, edited Peter Davey, Oxford, 1980.

Edinburgh

Edinburgh Tobacco Pipe Makers and their pipes. Dennis B. Gallagher & Andrew Sharp, Edinburgh, c.1986.

Glasgow

Glasgow, the tobacco trade and the Scottish Customs, 1707-1730. Jacob M. Price, in Scot. Hist. Rev. vol.63, 1984.

The Tobacco Lords of Glasgow.   Tom Devine in History Today.
        vol.40, 1990.

The Tobacco Lords, c.1740-1790. Tom M. Devine. Edinburgh,
        1975.

VETS

The British Veterinary Profession, 1791-1948. Iain Pattison,
        London, 1983.

The Veterinary Directory. [1861, 1967].

WARRANT HOLDERS

List of Royal Warrant Holders. [1930 - 1938].

WEAVERS & THE TEXTILE TRADE

General

The   Scottish   Handloom Weavers,   1790 - 1850.   N.   Murray,
        Edinburgh, 1978.

The Scottish Linen Industry in the 18th century. Alastair J.
        Durie, Edinburgh, 1979.

Scottish spinning schools. Lochbroom, Lochcarron.   Irene
        F.M. Dean, London, 1930.

The Weavers Craft. Daniel Thomson, Paisley, 1902.

The   big cloth.   The history and the making of Harris Tweed.
        Mary Gladstone, 1981.

The Tweedmakers.   A history of the Scottish   fancy   woollen
        industry,   1600-1914. Clifford Gulvin,   Newton Abbot,
        1973.

The Paisley thread Industry. Mathew Blair, Paisley, 1907.

Records of British Industry, 1760 - 1914, Textiles &
        Leather. H.M.S.O., 1990.

Kelly's   Directory   of the Manufacturers of Textile Fabrics.
        [1880 - 1928].

Worrall's Textile Directory of the   Manufacturing   Districts
        of   Ireland,   Scotland,   Wales   and   the   counties of
        Chester, Derby, Leicester, Nottingham. [1889 - 1950].
        (Latterly   known   as ' British & Dominion   Textile
        Industry '].

Angus

Juteopolis: Dundee and its textile workers, 1885-1923.
        William M. Walker, Edinburgh, 1979.

History of the linen trade, ancient & modern.   A.J.Warden,
        London, 1864.

Dundee & its Textile Industry, 1850-1914. B.P. Lenman, Abertay Historical Society, Dundee, 1969.

The Dundee Textile Industry, 1790-1885. Enid Gauldie, Edinburgh, Scottish History Society, 1969.

Dunfermline

The weavers' craft being a history of the weavers' Incorporation of Dunfermline. D. Thomson, Paisley, 1903.

The Old Weavers' Drive. Martin Norgate, 1971. [contains accounts of weavers' outings and an appendix listing weavers who took part along with their addresses and year of birth.].

Edinburgh

The Weavers of Picardy. John Mason, B.O.T.O.E.C., vol.25, 1945.

Glasgow

Old Glasgow Weavers, 1514 - 1905. Robert D. McEwan, Glasgow, 1905. [A 3rd. edition continued by William Maclean: a 4th edn. revised to 1981 by Ian L. Dunsmore].

Excerpts from the records of the Weavers' Society of Anderston, instituted 1738. Glasgow, 1879.

Essay on the transactions of the Weavers' Association of Glasgow. C. M'Kay, Glasgow, 1829.

Haddington

The records of a Scottish cloth manufactory at New Mills, Haddington, 1681-1703. W.R. Scott, Scottish History Society, Edinburgh, 1905.

Hamilton

Hand-loom weaving in Hamilton & District. ed. C. Smith. Hamilton District Libraries, 1976.

Kilsyth

Weavers, miners & the open book. A History of Kilsyth. James Hutchison, 1986.

Perth

Perth: Its Weavers and Weaving. Peter Baxter, Perth, 1936.

Paisley

The Paisley Shawl, and the men who produced it. Mathew Blair, Paisley, 1904.

The Incorporation of Weavers of Stirling. David B. Morris, Stirling, 1926.

WHALING

Aberdeen & the early development of the whaling industry, 1750-1800. W.R.H. Duncan, in North Scot., vol.3, no.1, 1977-1978.

North-east Scotland and the northern whale fishing, 1753-1893. R.C. Michie, in North Scot., vol.3, no.1, 1977-1978.

WITCHES

A Source-book of Scottish witchcraft. Christina Larner, Christopher Hyde Lee and Hugh V. McLaclan, Glasgow, 1977.

A Calendar of Cases of Witchcraft in Scotland, 1510-1727.

Enemies of God. Witchcraft in Scotland. C. Larner, London, 1981.

History of Witchcraft in Scotland. C. Kirkpatrick Sharpe

Scottish Witches. Charles W. Cameron, Norwich, c. 1984.

Witch Hunt, The great Scottish witchcraft trials of 1697. I. Adam, 1978.

Witchcraft in South-West Scotland. J. Maxwell Wood. Reprint 1975, Wakefield.

Witchcraft & Second Sight in the Highlands & Islands of Scotland. John Gregson Campbell.

Trials for witchcraft. John Strathauchine. Spalding Club Misc. 1, Aberdeen, 1841.

Notes on cases of Witchcraft, Sorcery, 1629-1662. Spottiswoode Society Misc., 1845.

A Historical account of the belief in witchcraft in Scotland. Charles Kirkpatrick Sharpe, Glasgow, n.d.

Witchcraft in British History. Ronald Holmes, London, 1974.

Aberdeen

Trials for witchcraft at Aberdeen, 1596-1597. J. Stuart, Miscellany Old Spalding Club, vol.1, 18401.

Alloa

The Witches of Alloa. R. Menzies Fergusson. Scottish Historical Review, vol.4, 1907.

Angus

Tay Valley Witch Trials. Michelle Merrick, Tay Valley Family Historian, no.17, 1987.

Dumfriesshire

Unpublished witchcraft trials. A.E. Truckell, in Trans. Dumfries & Galloway Nat. Hist. Antiq. Soc., 3rd. ser. vol.51, 1975.

East Lothian

Witch hunting in East Lothian. East Lothian District Library,, 1976.

Fife

The 17th century witch craze in West-Fife: a guide to the printed sources. Chris Neale, Dunfermline, 1980.

Inverness-shire

The witches of Badenoch. Niall M. Brownlie, Scots. Mag., vol.121, no.4, 1984.

Kenmore

Witchcraft in Kenmore, 1730 - 1757. John Christie, Aberfeldy, 1893.

Kinross-shire

Witchcraft in Kinross-shire. R.B. Begg. Kinross, n.d.

Renfrewshire

The Witches of Renfrew. Ann Mackay, Scots Mag. vol.128, 1987.

History of the witches of Renfrewshire. J. Millar, Paisley, 1809. New ed. with additions, 1877.

Stirlingshire

The witches of the Ochils. Rennie McOwan, Scots. Mag., vol.122, 1984.

WOOD-CARVERS

Carvers in restoration Scotland. John Greenwell Dunbar, in Country Life, vol. 162, 1977.

WORKHOUSES

The History of the Workhouse or Poors Hospital of Aberdeen, 1739 - 1818. [then the history of seperate hospitals up to 1885]. Aberdeen, 1885.

WRIGHTS

Dundee

The 3 United Trades of Dundee: masons, wrights, slaters.
Annette M. Smith, Abertay Historical Society, 1987.

Glasgow

The Incorporation of Wrights in Glasgow. 4th ed. James A.
Reid, 1900, Glasgow.

Kirkcaldy

Incorporation of Wrights' Benefit Society of Kirkcaldy.
Sheila Campbell, Scott. Genealogist, vol.33, 1986.

A DICTIONARY OF EDIN CABINET.

FRANCIS BAMFORD 1983

Sc. Genealogist v 39 no 2. 1A. D. TORRANCE.

FURNITURE
Some EDIN. ~~FURNITURE MAKERS~~ MAKERS

F. BAMFORD. B O T O E C.
vol 33. 1966
ED. BRANCH
of Sc. Most Union of Cabinetmakers.
1833 - 837.
B O T O E C vol 3(6) 1969

MURRAY -
LADY GLENOREN'S CHURCH (member) were F.M.
JAMES MURRAY 1993 JOINER.

WILLIAMSON'S EDIN DIRECTORY 1811/12 1830?